TH

LOVE
PRISON
MADE

AND UNMADE

THE
LOVE
PRISON
MADE

AND UNMADE

My Story

EBONY ROBERTS

AMISTAD

An Imprint of HarperCollins*Publishers*

HarperCollins books may be purchased for educational, business, or sales promotional use. For information, please email the Special Markets Department at SPsales@harpercollins.com.

Some names have been changed in this book to protect people's privacy.

FIRST HARPERCOLLINS PAPERBACK EDITION PUBLISHED IN 2020

Designed by Joy O'Meara

Library of Congress Cataloging-in-Publication Data is available upon request.

ISBN 978-0-06-287665-2

20 21 22 23 24 LSC 10 9 8 7 6 5 4 3 2 1

To Sekou,
for reminding me that love is
the greatest healer

Love recognizes no barriers. It jumps hurdles, leaps fences, penetrates walls to arrive at its destination full of hope.

—MAYA ANGELOU

AUTHOR'S NOTE

I looked up to the Black couples I read about. Like Malcolm X and Betty Shabazz. Like Ossie and Ruby Dee. Like Kathleen and Eldridge Cleaver and Winnie and Nelson Mandela. Theirs was a love rooted in the Black struggle for liberation. A love that had purpose. I wanted to have what I called a Black power fairy tale. So when I found Shaka, a brother who reminded me of Malcolm and Eldridge and Mandela, I fell in love. Never mind he was locked up.

But, this story started long before I met Shaka. It started in the cradle of my parents' marriage. It is there that I learned what women must do for the sake of having love and what we must do to keep it.

1

grew up fantasizing about my knight in shining armor. There were white knights and white horses and white picket fences in the books I read and I bought into the hype. But my knight was a Black boy.

And I was a Black girl trying to find my way in a world that assaults Black girlhood before we even become women, that tells us the fairy tales we read aren't for us. I longed to be saved by a boy who would love me, who would fight for me, who needed me as much as I needed him. A boy who would give me happily-ever-after.

I didn't know any Black girls with real-life Black fairy tales and happily-ever-after endings. Not even the Black girls on TV had happy endings. But that didn't stop me from dreaming. Then *The Cosby Show* aired, giving my nine-year-old self a peek into a Black world that was abundant.

The Cosby Show was as far from reality for me as white horses and white knights, and I was captivated. The Huxtables weren't poor like the Evans family, and the children weren't adopted like Arnold and Willis. Cliff and Claire Huxtable were idyllic parents and the perfect couple, living the American dream. I envied Theo and Vanessa and Rudy, who had everything I didn't have. I wanted their scripted lives.

I even envied J.J. and Thelma and Michael. Though their project apartment was worlds away from the Huxtables' Brooklyn brownstone, their parents clearly loved each other.

Sometimes I couldn't tell if my parents even liked each other.

At home one day, sitting in the living room pretending to watch television, half listening to my mama and daddy argue in the dining room, I heard my mama say calmly, "Bill, put that away." I turned from the TV to see my daddy pointing a gun at my mama, her eyes wide with fear.

It wasn't the first time I'd seen Daddy's pistol, but it was the first time I'd seen it pointed at anyone. Mama looked at the gun and then back up at him. He stared right through her. "I ain't putting shit away," he snapped, tightening his grip on the .357 Magnum as he planted his 5'5" body firmly into the floor. His eyes were red with rage and his already pale skin looked more pallid. He grinned at her as she pleaded.

"Please, don't do this," Mama cried, inching backward toward the front door, her eyes locked on the gun. Fear rose in my chest. My twelve-year-old eyes watched, my mouth wide open, as Daddy lifted the pistol more. Higher and higher the mouth of the gun rose, meeting Mama's eyes.

Without a word, she turned and bolted toward the door. He followed behind her, chasing her out of the house.

I jumped up and ran behind him, screaming, "Daddy, don't!" I screamed and screamed some more, then fell to the vestibule floor as he pushed opened the screen door, pleading with him, "Please don't! Noooo . . ."

He ignored my cries. His anger, or maybe it was the vodka, made me invisible to him.

And then, "Boom!" The gun exploded with gunfire.

The sudden sound of the bullet leaving the gun's chamber echoed in my ear. I rushed outside. Time slowed as my eyes scanned the front yard, frantically searching for my mama. When my eyes finally found her, she was halfway across the street running toward our neighbors' house, her bare feet slapping against the hard concrete. The bullet had missed her. My daddy stood on the porch watching her run to safety, still cursing her. I stood beside him, tears streaming down my face.

That day, I retreated further into my shell. I found sanctuary in books and Black family sitcoms and vowed to find a love I didn't have to run from.

My parents were high school sweethearts. She was fourteen, he fifteen when they met at the Graystone Ballroom, one of Detroit's most storied musical landmarks. Teenagers gathered there every Sunday afternoon to dance to the Motown sounds of The Supremes, The Temptations, and The Miracles. It was my uncle, Sherman, my daddy's younger brother, who introduced them.

"I wish you had a taller, older brother," my mama joked with Sherman.

He didn't say a word. He disappeared into the crowd of

dancing teenagers, and moments later returned with Daddy. Mama says she wasn't impressed. Daddy was older, but he was short and almost white with straight, dark hair. A pretty boy. Mama didn't like pretty boys but she smiled and told him her name. "I'm Carolyn," she said over the music.

"Name's Bobby," he lied.

They talked and danced and then exchanged numbers. Daddy called her the next day and they made plans for him to come over on Wednesday. They sat on the tattered sofa in her family's front room and gabbed about school and music, her mama in the next room within earshot. He visited every week and charmed his way into her mama's, my grandmother's, good graces, bringing her a strawberry Faygo, her favorite soda, every time.

Each week Daddy showed up in a different car he had stolen pretending to be a valet at Joe Muer Seafood, an exclusive whites-only restaurant near downtown Detroit. He would lie to Mama whenever she asked about the cars. "That's my cousin's car," or "That's my friend's car," he'd say with a straight face.

Over time, he grew on her, cracking jokes and spoiling her with gifts he'd stolen from his mama's Avon orders. Later that year when Mama's mama died, Daddy was right by her side. "What you want to do?" he'd ask, and then take her wherever she wanted to go.

They started talking marriage after Mama finished school. That's what young couples did in the sixties—graduated high school and got married. But after asking her father's permission, Daddy found reasons why they weren't ready, so Mama broke things off and moved to North Carolina.

Daddy called her almost every day, trying to get her back, and by the following June, they were married. It was 1967 and the United States was two years into the Vietnam War. Daddy was drafted months later and sent across the country to an army base in Tacoma, Washington, with Mama by his side. He ended up being one of the lucky few who never went to Vietnam.

Daddy strayed early and often. Mama knew about the other women, but she stayed. She'd grown up in a big, loving family and wanted what her parents had. They raised eleven children together—six girls and five boys—and were married until my grandmother's death. My grandfather worked on the assembly line at Ford, a good factory job that took care of his family. He'd fled the racial terror of the South in the 1920s like many Black men, first moving to Chicago, and then Detroit. Whatever he ran from, he never spoke of and he forbade his children from going south. But Mama didn't heed his warnings. Once she and Daddy married, she went with him to Mississippi nearly every year to visit his people.

I loved when Mama told me stories about her childhood. She told me about the chili my grandfather cooked every Saturday. She told me how my grandmother loved it when she greased her scalp, how my grandparents loved her, their baby girl, and her siblings with a gentle hand. She told me how my aunts, who were nine years older than her or more, gave her whatever my grandparents could not. She told me how, when my daddy asked for her hand in marriage, my grandfather asked him if he cared about my mama, his daughter, and Daddy said,

"No, I love her." That was the wrong answer, Mama told me. After forty years of marriage, my grandfather knew love wasn't enough.

Just four years into their young marriage, my parents broke up and the house they bought together as newlyweds went into foreclosure. Mama had planned to move in with my grandfather until she found an apartment of her own and Daddy planned to stay with a friend, but days before they were to move, Mama found out she was pregnant. They decided to try to make their marriage work. The next year, they had a boy and named him after my daddy, but spelled his name Billy instead of Billie, the way Daddy's was spelled.

The baby changed nothing.

Two years later, although Mama didn't have any hopes of my daddy straightening up, she decided she wanted another baby. "You were the fattest baby I'd ever seen," she told me all the time. "You slept so much I had to put a mirror up to your face to make sure you were breathing."

Now with two kids and a husband who didn't come home at night, Mama turned to food. She'd gain weight, he'd joke about the extra pounds, and she'd lose it, only to gain it all back. Then one day when I was four years old and my brother was seven, Mama packed a bag of clothes for herself, for me, and my brother, and we left. She'd plotted for months, saving what money she could for the first month's rent and security deposit on a townhouse in Royal Oak Township, a working-class suburb north of Detroit. Daddy didn't know where we were.

The cockroaches were merciless in the way they took over our two-bedroom townhouse. They crawled on the floors, on the ceilings, on blankets, and sometimes on me. No matter how many times Mama tried to get rid of the bugs, they returned.

After a few months, Mama broke down and told Daddy where we were. That became their pattern. Breaking up and getting back together. A year later, the four of us moved into a small brick ranch on the corner of Seven Mile Road and Marlowe, an established neighborhood on Detroit's west side with mature trees and large brick houses, some colonial, some ranch, but all much bigger than ours. The man who owned the Buick dealership just beyond our backyard also owned this house and rented it to us for $275 a month as a favor to my uncle, who worked for him.

Mama had prayed about that house. It only had two bedrooms but the neighborhood was nice and the rent was something she could pay on her own if things didn't work out with Daddy again.

2

I was a daddy's girl. Everybody said I looked *just* like him—fair complexion, wild, bushy eyebrows, and a space between our two front teeth so big it looked like they were never meant to be together. The only difference, his skin was so light and his hair so thin and straight that he could have passed for white. Not me, I had tight, nappy curls like Mama.

Daddy had a big heart and an even bigger personality. He was every bit country as he was city slick. He rode motorcycles and horses and would eat anything on four legs. He wasn't afraid of anything.

But me, I was afraid of everything. He'd always tell me, "Ah, you'll be all right," whenever I was unsure. He was my hype man, rooting me on as I pedaled down the street, bike wobbling, the first time I rode my bike without training wheels, or I hopped on the scariest rollercoasters, heart pounding, stomach in knots.

Whenever we visited my great-grandparents' Mississippi farm, I'd watch him, peeking through my little fingers, as he

slaughtered the animals that would be dinner. One time I remember him standing bare-chested and red from the sun with
a butcher knife in one hand and a beer can in the other as two
goats dangled from my great-grandmother's clothesline, squeal-
ing. Without ceremony, Daddy raised the knife and slit their
necks open. Blood gushed and squirted everywhere. Daddy
laughed in amusement, the sound of his laughter hanging there
in the thick Mississippi heat.

He was a man's man. He did what he wanted, when he
wanted, and he never took no for an answer. If he wanted
something, he got it, and if it didn't work out, he'd dust himself
off and get right back up.

I wished I could be that brave.

I wished I had been brave enough to say no when a family
member, someone I loved and trusted, led me into his dank,
dark basement. "I want to show you something," he said.

I followed him into the bathroom tucked behind the stair-
case. He sat down on the toilet and pulled me near. He told
me not to be afraid. I can still remember the smell of his musty
unwashed balls as he revealed his big, black penis to me and
told me to touch it. He smelled of dirty hair and cars, his hands
covered in oil from the engines he worked on. I did not say a
word. The words would not have come if I had tried.

My memory ends there. The screen in my mind goes black.
I replay the scene over and over and it always ends there. I was
five years old.

I didn't understand what was happening, but I knew it was
wrong. I knew because he took me into the basement, into
the half bathroom that no one ever used. I knew because he

whispered. I knew because my body froze when I saw his big, black penis standing straight up like a tree.

But I didn't tell my daddy any of this. I didn't tell anyone.

Those days, I didn't talk much. I was the quiet child. I watched and listened and tried not to get in the way.

By the time I was nine, resentment started to creep in. I don't know if it was because I was maturing and could see things for what they were or because Mama started telling me what Daddy was and wasn't doing, but the father I knew and loved was disappearing.

Daddy's drinking had gotten worse. Now there were seizures.

The first time I saw my daddy have a seizure I had gone with him to the liquor store. We were standing in line when his body suddenly started jerking back and forth. My body stiffened with fear as I watched him fall to the ground, his body still convulsing. "Put something metal in his mouth!" someone yelled. I stood there, helpless, as the bodies around me hurried into action. Someone grabbed his legs and tried to hold them down. Someone else held his head. "Step to the side, baby," a woman muttered to me.

I stared at his almost white body flailing against the almost black carpet, dirty from being stepped on so many times, my eyes fixed on his broken, erratic movements. Eventually, the shaking slowed then stopped. He laid there for a moment and then stood up as if everything were normal. He paid for the alcohol he'd come to buy and we left. We didn't say a word on the walk back home.

I don't know if the seizures were connected to Daddy's drinking, but it's all I ever saw him doing. Vodka or gin straight was his preference—and directly from the bottle. His eyes glassed over and red, he'd lay there on the couch half-sleep or half-watching television, sipping on the bottle all day. I wanted to help him. Tell him, "You've had enough." Sometimes I'd hide his liquor bottles. I knew better than to throw them away.

I was his babysitter on those drunken days, keeping my eye on him whenever he was home so I could call for help if he had a seizure, or help him if he stumbled and fell in a drunken walk from one room to another. I would watch him as he moved through the house, his steps broken and unsteady. When I could no longer see him, I'd listen for his feet shuffling against the carpet. Sometimes he'd stop and lean on the wall or the furniture and the shuffling would stop. "You okay?" I'd call to him. He'd mumble something, and I'd hear the shuffling again.

Daddy's thin, pale skin bruised easily, and I'd count the purplish-blue spots on his arms and legs. I'd ask him about the injuries I hadn't seen. "Daddy, what happened here?"

"Eh, I don't know."

Sometimes he'd show up to our school inebriated. "That's my baby," he'd say enthusiastically to anyone who would listen. I'd watch him walk down the halls trying to stand upright, pretending to be more sober than he was, smiling and nodding at other parents. But I could tell. His eyes always betrayed him. They told the story we all tried to hide.

I felt a mix of resentment and embarrassment whenever he came to our school events. I knew he was proud of me and my brother, but I didn't want him there. School was my refuge from the drama at home.

Mama kept me in the middle of their drama. She'd tell me about the problems they were having, how there was hardly enough money to pay the bills, how Daddy barely worked his factory job at General Motors. We'd sit at the kitchen table, her with a cup of coffee and a cigarette and me all ears, listening as if I were watching one of my favorite TV shows.

"I didn't get anything last week," she said as she flicked the ashes from her cigarette into the ashtray. "He didn't work. He said he was going to bring me some money, but I won't hold my breath. You know how that goes. If he comes, he comes. If he don't, I'll see if Joann can loan me a few dollars to get some groceries for the week. He said he wants to come back home, but I don't know. I ain't getting no child support no way, right?" She didn't wait for me to answer. "When people show you who they are, believe them," she continued. "That don't mean you gotta stop messing with 'em, but just know who you dealing with." She sipped her coffee and continued on like this for hours. I hung on to her every word.

Mama made just enough to pay the rent and buy staples for the house—bread, milk, eggs, beans. She'd borrow money from family to make ends meet, and sometimes my aunt Joann, who was a homemaker and more like a grandmother to me than an aunt, would make enough food for us when she cooked dinner for her family.

We weren't poor enough to get free lunch at school, however. Mama made too much, they said, so my brother and I got our lunches at a reduced price. My mama was grateful. I watched her go to work every morning, exhausted before her day had even begun, and come home every night more tired, not just physically tired from a hard day's work but weary from trying to hold our house together, from dealing with unforgiving supervisors who did not value her work, who watched over her shoulder, who spoke to her like she was nothing.

I was embarrassed. I hated school lunches. Only the kids who couldn't afford to bring their lunch from home ate them.

And I hated Christmas. It was always a reminder of how little we had. I don't remember ever believing in Santa Claus. Mama made it clear that it was her hard-earned money and sacrifices that bought any gifts we received. Whenever she got me something I *really* wanted, toys that were in great demand like the Cabbage Patch Doll or the Coca-Cola Polar Bear, I could see her smile with satisfaction when I opened my gifts, proud that she'd been able to get me what I wanted.

She tried to give us a childhood. She tried to make it work. But sometimes I just wanted her to leave Daddy alone so she could be happy, so she could stop worrying about the bills, so we could be free of the drama.

She was too tired to fight the court system, she told me. I imagine she was afraid of raising two children alone, of being unmarried and lonely.

Sometimes Daddy would stay gone for days. Linda was one of his girlfriends, the only one whose name I knew. She was brown, slightly darker than my mama, a woman with average, almost masculine beauty. On nights Daddy didn't come home, Mama would drive over to Linda's house looking for him. But she never got out of the car, she'd just sit there—me and her. We'd sit in silence, me in the backseat nodding, and her in the driver's seat fighting back tears.

When people started whispering about my daddy having another woman, Mama gave him an ultimatum.

"Either you gone be here, or you gone be there, but you can't keep coming and going in and out of this house."

"Well, I'm not gone leave her alone."

"Then get your shit and get out."

For days, Mama stewed, her rage building the more she thought about the choice he'd made. Eventually, on a cold Michigan night, she drove over to Linda's and this time she got out of the car.

"Open up the door, goddamit!" she screamed again and again as she banged and kicked on the front door. "You no good son of a bitch! How you gone choose that heffa over your family?" she continued, ramming her body into the door with superhuman strength.

The door flew open, finally, and she ran upstairs to the second-floor flat where Daddy now lived with Linda. Her anger, her blood boiled as she banged and kicked on a second door, which, just like the first one, surrendered beneath the pressure of her foot. She cursed him some more.

"Carolyn, you need to get out of here," Daddy insisted. "You need to leave."

"Get out here, bitch," she called to Linda, who was hiding in a closet, still and quiet.

Moments later, two police officers surrounded her. Someone had called the police. After calming Mama down, after hearing both sides of the story, the police asked Mama to leave. She agreed.

She had a gun on her that night, a small .22 caliber pistol she started carrying after she'd almost been robbed months earlier. She told the police officers about the gun as they sat with her in the patrol car waiting on her to gather herself.

"Ma'am, how long you been married?" one officer asked.

"Eighteen years," she replied through tears.

"You got any kids?" he continued.

She nodded.

"How many?"

"Two," she said, almost whispering.

"Are they good in school?"

"Yes, all A's," her voice mixed with pride and sadness.

"What about them kids? You see he don't care nothing about them, now you're going to make them motherless too? If you kill him, you going to prison and he gone be dead. Is that what you want?"

Tears streamed down her face as she thought about what could have happened.

I listened to her tell me this story days later. I wasn't with her that night. She told me about the gun, about Linda hiding in the closet, about the police. This is not the mother I knew. This is not love, I thought to myself.

looked forward to going to school every day. I had little else in
my life to look forward to—no afterschool programs or summer camps, no sports leagues or weekend activities. Those
programs weren't for children like me whose mamas lived paycheck to paycheck, just trying to keep their head above water.
Then there was the drama between Mama and Daddy. For
those seven hours, I didn't have to think about what was going
on at home.

The moment I got home from school, I turned on the television. I watched Black parents like James and Florida Evans
love each other. I watched Black children like Arnold and Willis Jackson get loved on by their rich white dad. I escaped my
world of drinking and yelling and secrets until it was time for
bed. Whether they were well-to-do like the Huxtables or poor
like the Evans family, their families were whole. I tried to tell
myself that at least I had both parents.

One day after my brother and I had gotten home from

school, Mama said, "You need to talk to someone, someone who knows what you're going through." She looked down at the floor, then back at us before she continued. "Al-Anon is a support group for the families of alcoholics." The next week, my brother and I go reluctantly, me with suspicion, him with adolescent indifference. It is cold and dark and I'd rather be at home watching television. I'd rather not talk to Someone.

The meetings are held at a church not far from our house on Marlowe. The neighborhood was mostly Black, but the church, a historic two-story building made mostly of stone, was largely white and had been for decades. Someone greeted us when we entered, and we were directed to a small library just beyond the sanctuary. Everyone looked at us as we took our seats in the wide circle. I stared at the floor as Mama made small talk with the woman sitting next to her.

The already still room became quieter. They were about to begin. A woman's voice rose from the silence. "We welcome you to the Westminster Al-Anon Family Group and hope you will find the help and friendship you need. We who live, or have lived, with someone who has a problem with alcohol understand like few others can. We, too, were lonely and frustrated, but in Al-Anon we discover that no situation is really hopeless. It is possible for us to find peace, even happiness, whether the alcoholic in our life is still drinking or not." The circle nodded in agreement. I didn't see any hope in our situation. Daddy was sometimes in my life, sometimes out, most of the time drunk. How could I find any peace or happiness in that?

Moments later the young people were led to a cavernous room in the basement of the church. This group of teens, including preteens like me, were mostly white except for me and my brother. I looked around the room. I tried hard to find a part of me, of my experience in their unfamiliar white faces.

The group leader, a twenty-something white woman, said she'd been where we are, said she understood the shame, the anger, the guilt.

"It's not your fault. You cannot control the alcoholic. It is their choice to drink." We were not alone, she reassured us. Then she ordered us to repeat after her. "I did not cause it, I cannot control it, and I cannot cure it." The group repeated. "Al-Anon is for you, not them."

I said nothing, not to her or anyone else. When it was my turn to speak, I passed.

The testimonies did nothing for the anger that bubbled beneath my quiet exterior. This is useless, I kept telling myself. I did not need help. *He* needed help. Fix him and I would be okay. Fix him and our family would be whole again.

I did not know I needed the fellowship, or the emotional support. I was too young, too guarded, too hurt to appreciate what the group could do for me. They were strangers. How could these white people with their rehearsed stories and toothy smiles help *me*, I thought. So I held on to the pain. I buried it, never speaking to my mama or my brother or anyone else for that matter about the sadness or the anger.

We never went back.

Daddy tried once to get sober. He must have tired of chasing the bottle every day. Maybe he knew the toll all the drinking was having on his body, on us. I don't know why he tried, but it is enough for me that he did.

He admitted himself into an inpatient treatment program. I don't know what he did there—we didn't visit or talk to him— but he returned two months later sober and bearing gifts he'd made for me and my brother. He was proud of himself. And he looked well. His cheeks were full. His beer belly was smaller. He looked the best I'd seen him look in years. I saw glimpses of the daddy I once adored, the one who could fill a room with his laughter.

Some nights I would set the dining room table and drag my family away from the television, so we could eat dinner together like I saw the families on TV do. The only Black family I knew in real life that ate dinner together at the table was my aunt Darlene whose husband was a Black doctor with his own practice like Cliff Huxtable. It felt strange not eating in front of the television whenever I spent the night at their house. It almost didn't seem right. At dinner, they would ask my cousin Mark questions about his day, and me questions about my world, a universe away from their five-bedroom house with its circle driveway and in-ground pool.

Setting the table was strangely satisfying. None of our dishes or silverware matched but that didn't matter. I'd fold our thin paper towels like the cloth napkins at Red Lobster and imagine our mismatched plates were fine china. I'd attempt to start a conversation, but the dialogue was forced, like pages from a poorly written script.

"How was your day?" I'd ask, going around the table like they did on TV.

"Good," they'd say and then stare at their plates.

We'd rush through our meal and return, all of us, to the TV to watch the drama of other people's lives.

Thursday nights were our favorite. On Thursdays we entered the homes of the Huxtables and the Keatons, the white middle-American family in *Family Ties*. We laughed and laughed at the teenage struggles of free-spirited Denise Huxtable and conservative Alex P. Keaton. I treasured those nights, piled on the couch together, close as we'd ever been. My brother would lay on Mama's side, and I'd lay on top of him, Daddy sitting on whatever part of the couch was left. We'd watch with the volume up, drowning out the sound of police sirens and music booming from someone's car speakers driving down Seven Mile.

It wasn't perfect, but at least we were all together.

One day Daddy came home and showed me an ID that said STUDENT across the top. "Look at this," he said, beaming with pride, with promise. He'd enrolled in classes at the University of Detroit. I'm not sure what he'd planned to study but that would be his only semester.

Things were normal for a while, until they weren't. The bottle, or maybe whatever pain he carried but never named, had a hold on my daddy he couldn't shake. The drinking started again, and then the arguing.

The day I watched my daddy point a pistol at my mama, almost killing her, watching her run to save herself, was the day I lost whatever compassion for my father that remained. I gave up hope for him, for my family.

4

On April 1, 1988, just months after Daddy pulled the pistol on my mama, Mama woke me up in the middle of the night. "Your father's gone," she said. I waited for her to crack a smile, to say she was joking, but her face was serious. "They found him at Maymo's," she continued. My great-grandmother had moved to Detroit when my great-grandfather, Sand Daddy, died some years earlier. My daddy sometimes crashed at her house, or my grandmother's, if he wasn't with a woman.

I stared at Mama for a full minute, maybe more. I didn't know what to say. He had just turned forty. I walked around all day expecting, hoping for someone to shout, "April Fools!" No one ever did.

I don't recall what happened next, only that I did not cry. I did not mourn like everyone else around me. A week later, at the funeral, I sat in the front row staring at Daddy's still body in the steel blue casket that my grandmother picked out, his face darker in death than it had ever been in life, the makeup two shades too dark for his pale skin. I listened to the adults tell stories about him. I do not know if my heart was broken or numb but their stories did not move me. Their tears did not move me. A pastor, who I'm almost certain did not know my daddy because I'd never seen Daddy set foot in a church or say a word about God or Jesus, did his eulogy. He told the room to live right so we could go to heaven. I wondered whether Daddy had gone to heaven or hell.

For the rest of the day I went through the motions waiting for it all to be over.

The next day, I went to school and I did not say a word to anyone about my daddy's death. It was just another day. I did not want to talk about it. I did not want the sympathy. I was twelve with a pain I couldn't understand.

Maybe if I had told my teachers, or my classmates, not just that he had died, but that he was an alcoholic and had almost killed my mama, maybe then they would have understood why I hardly ever spoke, why I was so guarded. But I said nothing. That way there would be no prying, no questions into how he died, no comments about how young he was and how sorry they were for me and my brother. I didn't want them to know I was relieved. I was happy the drama was over.

After Daddy died, Mama became more protective. That summer, I turned thirteen and the hips I inherited from her started getting attention. She skipped over the birds and the bees and went straight to the talk about babies. "I'm just letting you know, I ain't raising no babies," she told me more times than I can count.

When I met Will, the first boy who liked me, she kept a close eye on us. Will was my cousin Dana's friend and a "bad boy" like my daddy. He was fifteen and sold drugs. He had the color and the face of LL Cool J with full lips that he licked often. He knew my mama was watching him whenever he came around, so he was always respectful—he never tried to kiss me or feel on me, though I wanted him to. I wanted to see for myself what the girls at school talked about. I'd never been kissed, and I could tell he knew his way around a girl's body. He was cool and indifferent in the way boys in the hood can be, and whenever he came near me my body got warmer.

Dana was seventeen and trying to be a thug, but he'd been raised by my very religious aunt Ruby and didn't have the edge Will had. Mama was Dana's favorite aunt and when she'd pick him up to go shopping or to the movies, Will would come too. We hung out almost every weekend the summer before I headed to high school—me, Mama, Dana, and Will. We'd usually end up at the dollar movie, and in the dark theater Will and I would hold hands. His hand, warm and clammy, stayed glued to mine the entire movie, hidden from the watchful eyes of my mama.

When school started, Will moved to the east side of Detroit, a world away from my westside home, a world I mostly knew through the grim pictures my mama painted. "The east side is *rough*," she'd warn me. It's where Black families first settled when they migrated from the South during the Great Migration, but it's also where heroin, and later crack, hit the city the hardest.

Will and I talked on the phone almost every day. "When am I going to see you again?" he kept asking me.

I never did.

Will killed himself in a game of Russian roulette. My heart ached. He had lived a tragic life, cycling in and out of the streets, in and out of foster homes. At the time, I didn't understand why he'd play such a disturbing game. I didn't have the tools then to unpack what it meant to be Black and a boy, the daily assaults on his growing manhood, the oppression that squashed whatever life he had eked out living a hard, fast life in the streets. I wished I could have saved him.

That fall, in my ninth-grade English class, we read Maya Angelou's *I Know Why the Caged Bird Sings*. I was reminded of what happened to me in that dank basement bathroom when I was five. I read and reread Angelou's words. "He threw back the blankets and his 'thing' stood up like a brown ear of corn. He took my hand and said, 'Feel it.'" Something like shame came over me. I buried my secret even deeper.

I did not trust love, yet I wanted someone, a boy, to love away the hurt.

I met Dre in Physical Science. He reminded me of Will. They were about the same complexion, same height, and Dre was a bit of a bad boy too. He came from a two-parent home, probably wanted for nothing, but he hung out with his friends from the hood, smoked weed, and sold drugs. He had more confidence than I'd seen in a boy; his walk, the smooth way he talked evidence of his coolness. When he stepped to me, I was immediately taken. I loved his mannish ways, the way he pulled my body close to his when we kissed or lost his hands in my pants whenever we were alone. I didn't care in that moment that I wasn't the only girl he did these things to.

Eventually we started skipping school together, sometimes catching the bus to Fairlane Mall to hang out. We'd usually catch a movie and I'd let him kiss me on my neck. He'd pull up my shirt and suck on the tender flesh of my breasts, marking my chest with purplish-red marks. Every so often, the bright light of the movie screen would shine down on our seats, threatening to tell on us in the half-empty theater. I'd come home smiling, with passion marks in places my mama couldn't see.

I desperately craved Dre's attention and he gave it to me in small intense doses. I would page him and wait by the phone for him to call me.

One day I found out Dre had been arrested for armed robbery and sent to juvie. I was worried about him the whole time. When he was released, I listened to him tell me how his mama and daddy were trippin'. I wasn't able to save Will. Maybe I could save him, I thought. So I asked my mama if Dre could live with us. "Have you lost your damn mind?" she asked.

Mama didn't want me getting too serious about a boy because girls who focus on one boy fall in love and start having sex. And having sex leads to babies. I half-listened to her go on and on about what boys really wanted and what they did when they got what they wanted. "Don't you be no fool," she told me.

But I wanted what the boys wanted.

Just two months shy of my sixteenth birthday, against Mama's warnings, I got what I wanted. His name doesn't matter because he was just a stand-in for who I really wanted to have sex with. I really wanted Dre, but he was a player and I didn't want to get more emotionally attached than I already was. Half following Mama's warning, I decided to give my virginity to somebody I didn't care about. I had virginal dreams of slow, poetic lovemaking, but I chose a guy who could give me none of that. We had just started dating and I only kind of liked him. I invited him over on a day we had a half-day of school. It made no difference to him that I was a virgin. I was just another teenage conquest.

We didn't say a word to each other on the long, slow walk to my bedroom. Once we got to the bed, I took a deep breath and unbuttoned my shorts. I didn't get completely undressed and neither did he. We kissed awkwardly, and then I laid down on the bed, signaling that I was ready. He pulled a condom out of his pocket, slid it on, and then climbed on top of me. I braced myself for the pain, my body tensed as he entered me, the sound of agony stuck in my throat. He grunted and moaned, and I lay there in silence. I remain, in my memory, stiff and unwelcoming. It was as painful as my friends had described, blood and all. Then he came.

When he pulled out, my heart sunk. The condom had broken. Fear rose in my chest.

"I'm not raising no babies," I heard my mama say.

I jumped up like I was on fire and ran to the bathroom, thinking, hoping if I took a shower, if I stood up, the semen would fall out of me and wash away down the drain. I could not get pregnant.

A few months earlier, I'd asked my mama to take me to the doctor, so I could get on the pill.

"Are you sure?" she asked, stunned, worry in her face.

I waited in the clinic lobby with Mama for what seemed like forever. We were the only two in the room besides the receptionist. There was nothing but silence between us, then the nurse called my name, "Ebony Roberts."

I took a deep breath, stood up, and walked alone to the exam room.

"Are you sure?" the white middle-aged doctor asked me after talking to me about my options. I started having second thoughts. I chickened out. Maybe he was right, maybe I wasn't ready.

But I was.

Luck won out—no baby. When I finally had sex with Dre later that year, I didn't feel any different. My heart didn't flutter. My plan had worked. I tried to erase the memory of my first time and just enjoy sex with Dre, but I couldn't. I fixated on the condom, watching him go in and out of me.

The next day, he wrote on my locker, "Dre was here." Hurt and embarrassment welled up in me. But days later, he was at my house again.

I toggled between the good girl Mama wanted me to be and the bad girl I wanted to be. I wanted the freedoms my friends had so I quietly rebelled. I skipped school and made out in hallways and backseats, living as close to the edge as I could without my mama finding out.

One day at the mall with my best friend, Lisa, I tested the boundaries.

I pretended to show interest in a rack of shirts while Lisa went into the dressing room. I started getting warm when a girl about our age approached me.

"Can I help you find anything?"

Images of us getting caught flashed through my mind. "No, I'm just looking," I replied, trying not to sound nervous.

Lisa was in the dressing room for what seemed like forever, but after two minutes—the time it took her to take her baggy men's jeans off, put the denim Girbaud shorts on, and climb back into her jeans—she came out.

"I don't like the way they fit," she said as she laid a second pair of shorts back onto the display.

I pulled my book bag closer to my body. "Okay, you ready to go?"

"Yeah, let's go."

We didn't look at each other again until we left the store. Once we merged into mall traffic, I asked nervously, "Did you do it?"

"Yup," she smiled.

Encouraged by how easy it was to walk out of the store unnoticed, we decided to try again, this time at the department store Hudson's. Lisa agreed to go into the dressing room and do what she did in the other store.

We headed straight to the men's department. Lisa and I wore oversized men's jeans and shirts like the girl group TLC. We found a table full of striped denim shorts and looked for a pair that didn't have a theft protection sensor.

"I found one," Lisa whispered.

I smiled. It felt like we'd hit the lottery. I waited outside the dressing room, and when she finished, we walked out of the store.

"Excuse me," a man called behind us.

We turned as two men dressed in plain clothes approached us.

"We saw you on camera," the taller one said.

Shit, I thought to myself. Lisa and I looked at each other and then at the two men. Our shoulders fell in defeat.

The men led us back into Hudson's and through a maze of doors that hid the innards of the 537,000-square-foot store, the places off limits to the public. They sat us down in a small room with bare white walls and a mirror. We said nothing.

For the first time since my daddy died, I wished he was alive. I wouldn't have to steal shorts at the mall. I don't know where Daddy got the money, but if my brother and I asked him for anything, we got it.

"What school do you go to?" one of the men asked.

"Renaissance," I answered.

"What are you two doing in here shoplifting? I know your parents would be hurt to hear you were trying to steal a pair of shorts." He and his partner talked to us for about 20 minutes and then let us go.

Even more than wanting my father alive, I wanted my mother to let me live. Free to make mistakes. Free to love who I wanted to love.

I didn't want to be a good girl anymore.

5

One dark winter morning, when Mama was long gone to work and my brother and I were getting ready for school, I heard a knock at the door. I peeked through the door's small window and saw the whites of a man's desperate eyes staring back at me. My heart started pounding. I said nothing. I stepped back from the door, hoping the eyes hadn't seen me.

Then the knock came again. I stood there frozen, thinking of what to do next.

Seconds later, I heard glass shattering in the basement. I screamed.

"What? What happened?" my brother stammered as he ran out of the bathroom.

"Somebody just threw something through the basement window," I explained, my heart beating faster.

We waited a few minutes, listening for movement in the basement. Nothing. "I think your scream scared him away," my brother said trying to comfort me.

I immediately called my mama at work. Within weeks we had armored bars on every window and door in the house. We were in prison. We could not look out the window without a reminder that we were not safe. No one was safe. Crack had arrived. It hit the city like a tornado, destroying lives and wiping out full blocks. On some streets, houses were either burned out, boarded up, or crumbling from neglect. Eventually, those houses were demolished, leaving empty swatches of land strewn throughout the city.

On our block, every house was still standing and still full of life, but at night we heard helicopters hovering overhead. Sometimes it seemed the helicopter was just above us, about to land in the middle of our yard. Lights as wide and bright as the sun beamed down searching the area for Black boys who were trying to escape the hood with the help of this new drug. I'd sit in my room and wonder who they were looking for, if it was anybody I knew.

If you didn't know someone who sold crack, you knew someone who used crack, and simple possession could get you life in prison—but only if you were Black.

The American government had long declared war on the Black community. They called it a war on drugs. They said they were trying to get drugs *out* of our communities, but we'd later learn they were responsible for bringing the drugs *in*.

This was the era when Detroit earned its reputation as the murder capital of the world. There were funerals before graduations, parlors filled with children too young to know death so intimately. On any given day, walking home from school or the corner store, you could get killed for your sneakers or your gold rope chain or leather coat. You could die in a drive-by, or any public place where an argument turned to shooting. Senseless murders are what the media called them.

A few months after my brother left for college, on October 6, 1990, the girl he went to prom with was killed in a drive-by shooting. Her name was Kya and she was an honor student who had just started her senior year of high school. I remember thinking how beautiful she was when I met her. Her hair was pulled back in a tight, slick ponytail, and as I remember it, she wore bright red lipstick. She reminded me of the singer Sade.

Kya's murder shook me. She was seventeen, two years older than me, and a good student like me. The shots were fired through the living room window as Kya sat waiting on her date who had stopped by a friend's house to show her off. She was shot three times, once in the head. She was the only victim, an innocent bystander caught in the crossfire between rival drug dealers. I remember staring at the newspaper, reading and re-reading her sister's words, "she was with someone she didn't know anything about."

No one was safe.

Mama used Kya's death as a cautionary tale. Don't date drug dealers. Don't go into anybody's house you don't know.

Two years later, months into my senior year, violence would hit close to home again. Rob, a guy my friends and I knew from the city's all-boys Jesuit high school, got into a fight at a birthday party, went to his friend's car to get a pistol, and shot and killed a man, an innocent bystander. I read every news story. TWO U-D HIGH STUDENTS CHARGED WITH MURDER the headline read on the front page of the *Detroit Free Press*.

My friends and I had been to parties just like that one where a fight over space or a look that lingered too long turned into a shootout and we had to run, scared and frantic, rushing toward the nearest exit. Whenever trouble started to brew—voices raised louder than the music, bodies pushing—we'd leave, trying to outrun the bullets that almost always followed. Later we'd find out the shooter was a friend of a friend of a friend.

Rob was a good kid, captain of the football team. He was sentenced to 10–25 years for second degree murder. We were on our way to college and he was on his way to prison.

No one was safe.

The fact that my brother and I made it through high school without incident—no babies, no bullets, no handcuffs—was no small victory.

6

The decision to go to college was almost made for me. I'd earned a full-tuition scholarship to Michigan State University in ninth grade and all I had to do was maintain a 3.0 GPA and earn a 21 or better on the ACT. I did both.

On the day I left for college, I had mixed emotions. I was ready to leave my mama's house, but I was leaving the only place I'd ever called home. My aunt and uncle drove me to East Lansing in their minivan, my mama seated in the back with me, holding back tears. Once we'd moved my things into my dorm room, Mama announced, "There's a box from me. Don't open it until we leave." I walked them down to the parking lot, and still holding back tears, Mama hugged me tighter than she'd ever hugged me.

That night I felt alone, but I'd wanted this freedom so I didn't allow the sadness to settle in. I opened up the box Mama told me not to open. It was a care package filled with goodies—a hodgepodge of pens, notepads, fingernail polish, candy, and my favorite, Better Made chips. I smiled, opened the bag of chips, and ate until there was nothing but crumbs.

I didn't go home on weekends, but I called Mama every Sunday. I told her about the things I was studying and the people I'd met. She told me about the drama on her job, like she always did. I'd listen for a few minutes and then tell her, "Ma, I gotta go." I didn't have to listen anymore.

That first year, I studied nationalism and Marxism, got baptized in feminist theory, and schooled on the politics of race. We read bell hooks and William Julius Wilson, dissected the *Federalist Papers* and the fall of the Soviet Union. One of my first assignments called for us to attend an event on campus and write about our experience. I heard Minister Khalid Muhammad, then national representative for the Nation of Islam and assistant to Minister Louis Farrakhan, would be on campus. I decided to go to the lecture.

When I walked into Erikson Kiva, I was immediately greeted by a young woman about my age. "As salaam alaikum," she said as she passed me a program. Her hair was covered with a navy blue headdress and she wore a knee-length navy blue dress with matching slacks underneath. Every door was guarded by Black men in suits and bowties, and on the stage there were more. A feeling of pride washed over me as I looked over the room. Black men in every shade of brown stood at attention, ready to defend the minister. I was used to seeing Black women on Sundays holding down the church doors, but this was nothing like that. This was the Fruit of Islam that Malcolm X had written about in his autobiography. The Nation's security.

The room was full of mostly Black faces. I found a seat in

the back of the lecture hall and watched as one speaker after another made remarks. When the minister took the stage, the room fell silent. "In the name of Allah, the beneficent, the merciful. All praise is due to Allah," he said, the cadence in his voice measured and sure. I watched the men in suits and bowties stare into the audience, their eyes scanning the room from left to right, then right to left. Their faces remained serious, unmoved by the minister's words.

"I've traveled all over the world and wherever the Black man is, he's at the bottom. No matter the social, political, economic system, you find whites on top and Blacks on the bottom. If it's a socialist country, you find the white socialist on top and the Black socialist on the bottom. If it's a communist country, you find the white communist on top and the Black communist on the bottom."

He was a modern-day Malcolm X. Just as fiery and unapologetic in his critique of white supremacy. I was captivated. I thought about the black-and-white footage I'd seen of Malcolm X speaking in churches and ballrooms about America's racism, about the lies that had been told.

Halfway through the lecture, half of the audience is on their feet, raising their fists, shouting in agreement. "That's right!" "Black power!"

I wanted more of that energy, that fire.

By the end of the night I learned that As One, the university's radical Black student organization, had sponsored the lecture. They invited the mostly student audience to come to their next meeting in the Union, and I did. It felt like I'd stepped into a meeting of the Black Panther Party. "Welcome, sister," everyone greeted me.

After that first meeting, I volunteered to be the secretary, and before the end of the semester I started volunteering with As One's weekly mentoring program, the Children of Malcolm X, which was held in nearby Lansing, where Malcolm X once lived as a child.

Some mornings we held study groups where we explored the work of Black writers like Chancellor Williams and Frantz Fanon. We probed and challenged one another.

"What is the role of the intellectual in a revolution?"

"Well, Fanon argues that the intellectual is nothing without the lumpenproletariat. That's where the force of any revolution lives. They are the majority. And they are the ones who have nothing to lose."

"What, then, does the intellectual do?"

"Awaken the lumpenproletariat."

"Decolonize their minds."

One night, a group of us, all freshmen, were on our way home from studying at our favorite off-campus coffee shop when a car full of rowdy white boys yelled, "Hey you fucking niggers!" as they drove by. The word landed like a live grenade in the middle of our group. We all turned, and the white boys, drunk with white privilege, laughed as if they owned us, daring us to say something.

"Who you calling a nigger?" someone in our group yelled back.

The driver slowed to a stop; five guys jumped out of the car and charged at us with fists raised. The three guys in our group, James, Luqman, and Bruce, stood in front of me and Kim and returned their punches. But they were outnumbered. Kim ran for help.

When James fell to the ground, two of the guys started kicking him in his head and stomach. Time slowed. I could hear a rush of air leave James's body each time a kick landed. I didn't know what to do. I wanted to jump on their backs, to punch them with all the strength in me, but all I could do was scream, "Get off of him!"

I had never seen, firsthand, the ugly, violent side of racism. I had seen the images from my mama's generation of police dogs and firehoses assaulting Black bodies, but this was not a picture I could eye from a distance and put away. This was not the violence I'd seen in Detroit.

The way that word rolled off their tongues, the way they charged at us, sent a message: We didn't belong there.

The reality of being Black on a predominantly white campus, of being a target of misdirected white rage woke me up. I imagined what it was like to face mobs of angry white people, throwing rocks and sticks and vitriol, and feeling powerless to stop it, to protect myself, fear and anger building inside. I never wanted to feel that way again.

When they had enough, the white boys stopped and jumped back into the car. Bruce and Luqman helped James up, who was bloodied and bruised, his glasses broken. He'd gotten the worst of the beating.

After that night, I never felt safe on campus. I knew that white folk could say and do what they wanted to who they wanted without impunity. I knew their privilege, and their high-paid white lawyers if needed, would get them out of whatever trouble they created.

That incident would be the last time I faced such overt

racism on campus, but I encountered white microaggressions almost daily.

"I don't see color."

"You're from Detroit? You're so articulate."

"Why does everything have to be about race?"

Kim and I lived in the same dorm and grew close after that night on the way home from the coffee shop. I'd never made friends easily. I didn't want anyone to know my family's secrets, so I never invited classmates to my house, not to do homework, not to hang out, and definitely not to sleep over. But Kim and I shared similar childhood experiences. We told wild stories about our family's shenanigans and did not have to explain, or apologize, for the foolishness. With her, I felt safe to just be.

Ninety miles away from home, in a space where I am no longer part of the majority, I clung to Kim, and to As One. They became my family.

7

When I learned how Black women had been conditioned over many centuries to hate ourselves, how Black girls like me had grown up thinking their hair was "bad" and straight hair like my daddy's was "good," I knew I could no longer perm my hair. I'd spent my childhood wishing I had my father's fine, straight hair. I'd be prettier, I thought. My grandmother would tell me how much I looked like my daddy, then say, "But you shole ain't get his hair." I knew what she was saying without her saying it.

Kim and I talked for months about cutting our hair. I'd stand in the mirror and pull my hair back in the tightest ponytail possible trying to imagine what I'd look like. I wondered if the back of my head was misshapen or I'd look like a boy.

One day, while I was working on campus for the summer as a camp counselor, Kim popped up. She'd done the big chop, cutting off all her hair, and was afraid to go home, anxious about how her mother would react when she saw her shoulder-length tresses gone. She'd driven straight from the barbershop in Detroit to East Lansing.

I was in awe when I saw her. I couldn't stop staring. Her head was perfectly round. Her skin, smooth and brown, was glowing.

"Kimmmm!" I screamed. "I love it! You make me want to get mine cut right now."

We laughed.

"Do it! You're gonna look so cute."

The next week, I did.

I sat in the chair almost frozen as my hairdresser cut handfuls of my hair. I didn't say a word as I watched the hair fall to the floor. When I heard the first buzz of the clippers, my heart dropped to my stomach. I closed my eyes once the cold steel teeth met my scalp and tried not to think about what I would look like when she finished.

"You ready?" she asked after more than an hour of cutting and clipping.

I held my breath as she made her final touches. "As ready as I'll ever be."

When she turned the chair around and I saw my short, natural hairdo for the first time, I grinned. I didn't look like myself. I looked regal. Almost instantly, my back straightened, my head leveled. I was a new woman.

Every day I looked in the mirror and studied my face—the shape of my nose, my eyes, the contour of my lips. I noticed details I hadn't paid much attention to. Before, whatever beauty I had I couldn't see it. I waited to be told I was pretty. Now there was nothing hiding my face. I felt beautiful for the first time.

8

Everything I knew about God I learned from my mama. Mama didn't have a church home, so that meant my brother and I didn't either, but she was a God-fearing, calling-on-the-name-of-Jesus kind of woman. Sunday was her day to rest, and if she did go to church, she usually fell asleep, me nudging her awake the entire service. Church was where she found peace, she'd tell me often. The only place she could rest.

The end of service, after the pastor preached but before the congregation was dismissed, was always uncomfortable for me. The pastor would ask, "Is there anyone here today who'd like to give their life over to Christ?" No one would stand. He'd ask a few more times, waiting for someone to meet him at the front of the church to be saved. This would go on for minutes. I felt guilty for sitting there, as if not standing meant the preacher hadn't done his job. One Sunday, after hearing his call at the end of service, I stood up. "Amen," I heard someone say. I was afraid of being left behind when Jesus returned, even though I didn't understand what that meant entirely. I just knew I didn't want to burn in a fiery hell for eternity.

Once I got to college, a whole new world opened up to me. I saw women wearing hijab and men with turbans. I had a friend who practiced Yoruba, a traditional African religion, and another who was a Rasta. I discovered that the world was bigger than Christianity, that there are hundreds of religions on the continent of Africa alone. I started doing the numbers. There are billions of people on this planet and thousands of religions. How could there be one pathway to God?

After I learned the truth about Christianity and American slavery, about the history they'd left out of my textbooks, I started to question what I'd been taught about God. I turned away from religion and decided to get to know God for myself.

As I completed one degree and moved on to the next, I started locking my short natural hair and read whatever self-empowerment books I could find. When I read Iyanla Vanzant's book *Tapping the Power Within*, I was fascinated. She described centuries-old African spiritual practices and discussed the power of recognizing and communicating with ancestral spirits. She recommended setting up an ancestral altar and explained how to do it.

Almost immediately, I built an altar in the bedroom of my grad school apartment with a small table, a white cloth, a white candle, an ankh (an ancient Egyptian or Kemetic symbol of life), and a glass of water. In the mornings, I sat before my altar and prayed. I called the names of my ancestors and asked them for protection and guidance as Iyanla had instructed. One day sitting cross-legged in front of my altar, I had a breakthrough.

I called my daddy's name, and for the first time since his death, tears started to flow. I whispered to him as though he were in the room with me, "I miss you, Daddy." I had never sat in thought about him long enough to feel anything for fear of what that vulnerability might stir up for me emotionally. I had closed my heart to him, memories of him fleeting. But I knew if I ever wanted to heal the pain of that loss, I had to feel the feelings I didn't want to feel, the ones I'd tried to numb as a child.

In that moment, I gave myself permission to cry for him, to miss him, and the tears felt good. I thought about the pain of losing him early, all the moments I didn't get to share with him, all the moments he would miss. I thought about the good parts of him. The way he was when he wasn't drunk, the way my family remembered him at his funeral, why he had so many friends, why women loved him, why Mama once loved him. I remembered our summers together on my great-grandparents' farm.

Every summer our family took a road trip to Newton, Mississippi. We'd leave Detroit after dark and my brother and I would sleep most of the way. We'd wake up to mountains on both sides and nothing but highway ahead of us. We sang along with Daddy to "She's a Bad Mama Jama," or his favorite, "You Dropped a Bomb on Me," for the rest of the 14-hour drive.

Once we turned onto Corinth, the long winding dirt road that led to my great-grandparents' house, I got butterflies in my stomach. I couldn't wait to see my cousins who I felt were lucky enough to live on the farm every day. We would roll into the red sandy yard, the crickets greeting us and the air already thick with heat, the Mississippi sun just rising. The moment

Daddy's Buick stopped, we stumbled over each other trying to get out of it. We would spend a week, maybe two, down south, but it always felt like we had spent the entire summer there playing in the red clay dirt, shelling peas, and feeding the hogs, chickens, and goats.

Maymo and Sand Daddy stood in the yard waiting as if they knew when we'd turned onto Corinth. They'd greet us with smiles and food. Acres of red dirt and crops stretched far behind their house. My brother, my cousins, and I would spend our days running around the farm, through the fields of corn and sugarcane, and climbing the red dirt hills. Some days we'd sit, the women and the girls, under the big pecan tree in their front yard on chairs aged and weathered from the Mississippi sun and shell black-eyed peas and crowder peas or snap green beans. The women would sit and talk about the food that had to be cooked, the chores that needed to be done around the farm, and us girls would sit and listen and learn the ways of women.

Daddy would spend his days drinking beer with his cousins and uncles. He seemed free, the way he threw back bottles of beer, laughing. He had been born in Mississippi in the 1940s but spent most of his childhood in Detroit. I do not know the struggles he faced, structural or otherwise, because he did not speak of them, but my college studies helped me to understand the things he did not say. That day, sitting in front of my altar, he became whole in my memory, a Black man, not just my father, but a man in a society that makes it hard to be Black. I cried for him and for me. I wished I knew then what I know now. If I had, I would have never stopped trying to save him. I would have never given up hope.

Mourning my daddy's death felt like I was betraying my mama. He was the bad guy. He'd hurt her. But I decided I could no longer carry her baggage and mine. Sitting there at my altar, I forgave him for not being who I wanted him to be. I cried and cried, and after an hour, I felt lighter. I felt free.

In this new space, a space that was uncomfortable, I grew. It was as if the Universe was watering me, sending me more books to read to feed the emptiness in my soul, to heal my broken heart. More books by Iyanla but also books on Black feminism and African spirituality and identity.

Three years later, after more than a year of research and writing, I successfully defended my doctoral dissertation. Family and friends drove up from Detroit in carloads and my brother flew in from New Jersey. Daddy would have been there too. He would have been sitting in the audience beaming with pride when I walked across the stage, telling anybody who'd listen, "That's my daughter." Maybe he would have sobered up for the occasion, for me.

By the time I graduated, I had no idea what I was going to do with my life. I could teach and do research, the reason I'd gone to graduate school, but that light started to dim the year I worked with a tenured Black professor who told me the truth about the academy. White men make the rules and the rest of us fight, sometimes nastily, for a seat at the table.

I had three options. I could apply for a tenure track teaching position at a major university, a job in the private sector, or a postdoctoral fellowship, which would give me more time to make up my mind. I decided on the last.

While I waited for decisions from Johns Hopkins University and the University of California–Berkeley, I started volunteering at a school just outside of Detroit, Nsoroma Institute. Nsoroma was an African-centered school that taught Black children—*African* children—about their history and culture, making Africa the center of the curriculum instead of Europe. I'd done my dissertation on African-centered teaching and had heard great things about the school.

When I met Malik Yakini, the director, we talked for more than an hour about my research and then he invited me on a tour of the school. "All the classrooms are named after ancient African cities or ethnic groups," he told me as we walked down the hallway. I saw TIMBUKTU, DOGON, ASHANTI, SERER on bright, colorful signs outside the rooms. We talked about how the classrooms were "liberated zones" where Black children could grow and learn free from the weight of oppression and anti-Black racism. I peeked into some of the rooms and the children sat in circles or small groups of four or six, bright-eyed and engaged. There were African artifacts and plants on the bookshelves, pictures of Black historical figures, and everywhere the colors red, black, and green. I was filled with pride as I watched the teacher in Zimbabwe, the Kindergarten classroom, read a picture book about Mansa Musa, an ancient king of the Mali Empire in West Africa. At the end of the tour, Malik told me to come back the next day to volunteer in Zimbabwe.

I was there every week. I met people who were vegetarian, like me, who were Muslim, who practiced Ifa or Akan, traditional African religions, or were still searching. I felt welcome, at home, among Black people who loved themselves, with their natural hair and dashikis and geles, smelling like Egyptian musk and frankincense. It was there that I discovered kale and falafel and learned the many ways to cook tofu—blackened, scrambled, barbequed. I felt reconnected to the people and places I'd loved in college.

I never wanted to leave, and neither did most of the parents or the students. It was evident in the smiles on the children's faces, the hugs from everyone I met, the soft greetings of peace. They were a family.

Malik became my brother though he was old enough to be my father. He'd come up in the radical seventies and made the nationalist ideas I'd studied in school real for me. He had a salt-and-pepper beard and long untamed locs like Bob Marley and was every bit a rebel. He wasn't a bad boy in the way Will or Dre were, but he was a risk taker, a rule breaker, unafraid to stand for what was right.

About a month after I started volunteering, I signed up for a leadership class Malik taught as part of the school's Community Education Program, which also offered African dance and African languages like Kiswahili and Medew Neter, the ancient language of Egypt (or Kemet as it was once known). We learned about Martin Delaney, who is known as the father of Black nationalism, and studied Marcus Garvey's Universal Negro Improvement Association and Elijah Muhammad's Nation of Islam. I began dreaming about building an institution of my own, one that would continue their legacies.

I was inspired by what I saw at Nsoroma, what I felt when I entered the classrooms. There were no early learning experiences like that in Detroit. I got to work immediately. I researched state licensing requirements, drafted a business plan, and started working on the curriculum. Whenever I saw children's books with Black protagonists, with brown faces and kinky hair—the types of books I never saw in my elementary class-rooms growing up—I bought them. I pictured three- and four-year-olds reading picture books with characters who had names like theirs, characters who explored faraway places they'd never heard of, and hoods they could relate to. I pictured these little geniuses eating snacks I'd made with the vegetables we'd grow together in our school garden and visiting Nsoroma for field trips.

Midway through the leadership class, Malik mentioned he was about to start a twenty-one-day juice fast. I was intrigued.

"Every year for the past twenty years, I fast for twenty-one days, a cleanse, leading up to the spring equinox. I start on March first and end on March twenty-first," he explained.

"That's so dope. I think I'm going to join you."

"Are you sure?" he asked, not certain I knew what I was signing up for. "Have you ever done a juice fast?"

"No," I admitted.

"Have you ever fasted?" he probed.

"Well, one year I observed Ramadan."

"This is different," he warned. "You won't be eating anything for twenty-one days. You'll just be consuming juice and water. Are you sure?"

I paused. I had a deep connection to food. There were the butter beans my grandmother made, my aunt Joann's corn-bread dressing, and the meals my great-grandmother cooked from scratch when we visited Mississippi. And there were the times Daddy cooked for us. Cooking was his love language. Some days he would bring home a raccoon or rabbit from God knows where, teeth and eyes still in its head, and roast it for dinner with big chunks of potatoes and carrots. The game was dark and greasy, and the smell was a distinct, musky odor, nothing like the beef or pork or chicken I knew.

One morning, after Daddy made breakfast, he called my brother and me into the kitchen to eat, the usual for a Saturday—eggs, sausage, biscuits.

"These eggs taste different," I announced after a few bites.

Daddy grinned. "Those aren't eggs. They're hogs' brains."

"Daddy!" I squealed. "That's gross!" I went on and on about how he'd tricked us.

He laughed until he was red in the face. "Ah, you'll be all right."

I smiled at Malik, and said, finally, "Yeah."

I bought a juicer and filled my refrigerator with a cornucopia of fruits and vegetables—apples, oranges, strawberries, carrots, kale, celery, beets. That first week was hard. I didn't like any of the vegetable combinations I tried, and I stayed hungry. Once I found juices I liked—carrot apple was my go-to—it got easier. I found strength I didn't know I had. By day twenty-one, I felt like I could do *anything*. If I'd disciplined myself to go twenty-one days without food, I knew I could do whatever I put my mind to.

Soon after I finished fasting, I learned I'd gotten the post-doc at the University of California–Berkeley, but I didn't want to leave Nsoroma. My work with the school fed me in ways I didn't know I needed. It gave me a sense of purpose, a sense of place. For the first time, I understood the Black struggle as a global struggle, one that stretched beyond America's borders. I imagined what our Black future could look like and I wanted to be a part of creating it.

Staying would mean turning down the postdoc I had waiting on me at Berkeley. It would mean giving up my dream of becoming a professor. If I accepted the fellowship, I would be able to continue the research I'd started with my dissertation, but I wouldn't be where the real work was, where my heart was—in the community.

A month before I was scheduled to move, after much prayer, I decided to stay in Detroit. No one understood my decision—not my mama, not my brother, and certainly not my dissertation committee. I'd just spent five years in grad school. I was on track to become one of the Black academic elite. But the moment I decided to stay in Detroit and work at the school full time, my spirit felt full.

9

Kim told me she was going to be on television, a telethon for a Detroit organization she'd started volunteering with a few months earlier. They were raising money to send books into prisons. When I turned on the TV, there was a light-skinned brother with neat cornrows sitting behind a table kicking it about all the issues that mattered to me—the so-called war on drugs, police brutality, mass incarceration. He looked Puerto Rican, or Black mixed with something else, and was part hood and part intellectual, passionate in his critique of racism and white supremacy. One personality after another came on appealing to the community. "Ninety percent of Michigan prisoners will be released at some point and most of them are returning to Detroit. It's up to us to determine how they come home—as predators or protectors." I wanted to get involved.

The organization met in the back of a Black bookstore on the city's west side, and I joined Kim at their next meeting.

The room was small with a large conference room table in the center that made it feel cramped. That night we wrapped copies of *The Autobiography of Malcolm X* in plain brown paper to send inside. Books have to be new without any writing in them, someone tells me as we work.

Over the next two months, we sent *When and Where I Enter: The Impact of Black Women on Race and Sex in America* by Paula Giddings and *Segu* by Maryse Conde to the hundred-plus men on our mailing list, but week after week, packages were returned to us, rejected by prison mailrooms. The reason they cited: the organization wasn't an approved vendor. But we weren't selling the books, and the copies were new, as required by policy.

Many of the men and women in prison can't afford to buy books, and if they have financial support from their families, the money is spent on basic necessities like toothpaste and deodorant and underwear. We knew this, the prison knew this, but our hands were tied. We learned that the only approved vendors were big box stores like Barnes & Noble and websites like Amazon and we refused to support the system that profits off prisons.

We stopped sending books and shifted our focus to families. With grant money we got from a county commissioner, we chartered buses and organized day-long trips to prisons across the state for families to visit their loved ones. I sent letters to the men on our mailing list. Tell your mama, your daughter, your wife to call us. For some, this would be their first time seeing their family in years, some for the first time since they got locked up. This is the way the system is set up—to separate families and keep them far away, so far that families have to scrape pennies together for a visit.

Between this work and my work at Nsoroma, I was busy. I managed correspondence from the men inside and communicated with families who called about our bus trips. I became one of the organization's six core members and the only woman once Kim stepped down to give birth to her first child.

One Friday evening Rashad, the light-skinned brother with cornrows I had seen on TV that day, called me out of the blue. He stumbled over his words telling me about something that could have waited until our next meeting. I had been feeling him for months, so I welcomed the conversation. I'd been drawn to him the moment I saw him dropping knowledge on TV, but working alongside him made my attraction grow. What started out as small talk turned into hours on the phone, and before we hung up, we made plans to hang out the next day. And then the next day. He was a writer, working for a local newspaper, and sometimes I accompanied him to events he had to cover. Before long I was spending nights at his house and we were inviting each other to family gatherings.

Rashad had done eleven years in prison for attempted murder, and like Malcolm X, turned his cell into a classroom, reading every Black history book he could get his hands on. He introduced me to the Republic of New Afrika and The Godfather trilogy and we kicked it for hours about the movement. I was in love.

Then one day I stopped by his apartment after a long day of work and noticed his bed was exactly as we'd left it the morning before. The creases in the blanket. The position of the pillows.

"You didn't sleep here last night," I told him.

"What are you talking about?"

"The bed. It looks the same."

He had spent the night at his ex-girlfriend's.

We never had the you're-the-only-one-I'm-seeing talk, but we were together nearly every day. I had a toothbrush there.

I cried for days. He was the first brother I dated who had similar ideas about politics and religion, who was as committed to the struggle as I was. I thought he was "the one."

Rashad said he wasn't ready for a commitment. He had caught the attempted murder case at nineteen and spent the prime of his life in prison. He said he'd missed out on a lot and had just gotten out of a relationship. I understood. But I didn't want to let him go.

My mama had tried to protect me from men like Rashad. She didn't like Will. She didn't like Dre. She didn't like any of the guys I liked. I don't know if she saw my daddy in them, but I knew Rashad was different.

I would wait until he was ready.

One day, out of the blue, Rashad told me to stand in front of the full-length mirror on the back of his bedroom door, naked. He wanted me to see what he saw, he said. He told me I didn't have any muscles because I was vegan. "Your arms are flabby. And see here and here, you got a lot of cellulite," pointing to my dimpled flesh, telling me what I already knew. I shrunk in shame.

At 135 pounds, I felt fat looking at my reflection in the mirror. I'd lost weight a year earlier on the twenty-one-day juice fast I'd done with Malik and loved my new slim figure. For the first time in my life I could fit into a size 6 jeans, and on a good day, a size four dress. But that day, looking in the mirror, I hated what I saw.

I started working out and reintroduced dairy and fish into my diet for more protein. I was at the gym five days a week, at least, for two hours. I lifted weights, I did cardio. I was determined to get rid of the cellulite.

A year later, I was firmer and leaner but the cellulite was still there, stuck to my body like glue. I was frustrated. I wanted to love my body. I wanted him to love my body.

If Rashad wasn't nitpicking my arms or legs, it was my clothes or my hair. "Your hair is scratchy," he told me whenever I tried to cuddle up next to him in the bed. I felt rejected, but I made excuses for him. He's a Scorpio, or he's just keeping it real, I'd say. I tried to convince myself that I'd rather he tell me the truth than lie.

We'd been dating, on again and off again, for about two years when Rashad randomly announced, "We should just get married."

I almost screamed with excitement. "Stop playing."

"I'm not. We can do it today." He worked downtown, and I was a 20-minute drive away. "We can meet at the city clerk's office."

I was giddy at the thought of finally having my dream family.

An hour before we planned to meet, Rashad called and said something came up at work and he couldn't make it.

Rashad and I continued to work together and continued to date. One night, at the end of one of our meetings, Rashad announced that the brothers at Carson City Correctional Facility had invited him and Terrence, a new member who'd recently come home from prison, to speak at their Black History Month program but Terrence's security clearance had been denied. "Anybody want to go up to Carson City?" he asked.

The room fell silent, and then the excuses came. I have to work. My son has a game.

"I'll go," I offered. I'd come to know the men's names on our mailing list like family. I'd talked to some of their mothers. They weren't just a prison number. I wasn't just a volunteer. Re-uniting families and sending books inside was my small part in the struggle. I wasn't much of a public speaker, but going inside to speak to the brothers was a natural next step.

I woke up before dawn that morning. Carson City was a two-hour drive from Detroit and the program was scheduled to start at 8am. It was dark and quiet outside when Rashad pulled up in front of my house. When I felt the cold winter air against my face I wanted to turn around and go back inside.

"What up doe?" Rashad said when I opened the passenger door.

"Good morning."

"You ready?"

"Yeah, but I might have to take a little nap before we get there," I joked.

The sun rose behind us as we drove through Ann Arbor and then Lansing. When we were about 20 miles from the prison, my stomach started doing backflips. This was my first time going inside. I stared out of the window as we drove down a long country road that hadn't seen many cars. Everything around us was gray and brown—the grass, the trees still empty from winter, the weathered old farmhouses surrounded by acres of land. We passed one farm after the other, each one almost identical to the last.

The closer we got to the prison, the more nervous I got. By the time we pulled into the parking lot, my hands had started sweating.

The prison looked like a college campus, except for the rolls and rolls of razor wire that hedged the grounds and the armed truck that patrolled the perimeter. The parking lot was empty. It would be another hour before visiting hours started and families from across the state piled into the lot, driving hours to see their son or father or husband. I got out of the car, stretched my arms, and inhaled the crisp winter air into my lungs. A faint smell of cow manure permeated the morning air, a familiar smell from my summers in Mississippi.

Inside, Rashad and I signed in and waited in the lobby, still and quiet, as if strangers. The bark of the officers' radios broke the silence. Then footsteps.

"Good morning," a voice called from behind us.

We looked up from our laps. "Morning."

"I'm Brad. Thank you for coming. The guys are excited to see you." Brad was the Special Activities Coordinator for the prison and had been our main point of contact.

"No problem. It's an honor," Rashad replied.

"We're going to be in the school building," he explained. "But first you need to be cleared through security."

I had imagined actual bars like I'd seen in movies—the heavy steel clanging shut, closing out the world with it. These doors were made of thick Plexiglas and were clear. Instead of a skeleton key, there was an officer sitting behind a Plexiglas window who controlled the movement of the doors with a button. Nothing happened without his authorization and no two doors could be opened at the same time.

"Lift your arms," a female officer ordered me. She patted my arms and then underneath my breasts. Her hands brushed along the lines of my body as I stood there like a statue.

"Here," another officer said, handing me what looked like a pager. "This is for your protection. If at any moment you feel threatened or unsafe, press this button. An officer will respond immediately."

Rashad and I were escorted out of one building and across the yard to the school building. The yard is quiet. Men in blue and orange coats amble from one building to the next. Brad leads us to a small classroom packed with black and brown faces. I stand there, taking in the room, thinking about the statistics I'd read over and over. One in every fifteen Black men is incarcerated. One out of three Black men will go to prison in his lifetime.

One of them could have been my daddy. I had been told stories about how he stole cars, once getting arrested for his involvement in an interstate auto theft ring. My brother told me, when he was about ten years old and I was seven, two men in black suits and a nondescript black sedan showed up at our house one afternoon and put Daddy in handcuffs. He was back home the next day.

I looked at the men, some young, some old, and wondered how they got there.

One of the organizers of the program, an inmate, greeted us

when we entered the room. He told us his name was Shaka. He was a serious figure with broad, muscular shoulders and long, untamed locs that framed his face. He was average height, but his confidence filled the room and made him seem much taller. We didn't shake hands—physical contact between inmates and visitors is forbidden. Rashad led the way, walking straight to the podium. I took a seat at the long table beside him.

Rashad had spoken in front of countless groups, but this talk was different. He was talking to his peers, men who walked the same prison yards he once walked. He knew they needed more than a feel-good pep talk.

"Brothers, this is no time for games. Them games is what got you sitting in here now. You better prepare yourself for what's on the other side of that time or you'll be right back in here. And that's what they want. They don't want you to raise your children. They don't want you to rebuild your community. They want you to give up." He challenged the men to step up and be accountable. "There's no room for excuses. I don't care if you never knew your daddy or your mama's on crack. You can do anything you put your mind to. Your future is up to you."

I watched as the brothers soaked up his words, their faces pensive.

When Rashad was done, Shaka opened the floor for questions. A middle-aged brother with glasses directed a question to me. "Sister, what do Black women need from Black men?"

"That's a good question." I paused. I thought about the men I knew in the community. Men like Malik and Rashad. "We need you to be present. We can't do this without you." I told them that we loved them, that we were rooting for them. They nodded and smiled.

My eyes found Shaka wherever he was in the room, but I tried not to stare.

When the program ended, the men thanked us. Juan, one of the other inmates who'd organized the program, reached to give Rashad a hug, and then me. I hesitated for a moment—we weren't supposed to have any physical contact. I didn't want to get him or us in trouble, but I didn't want to be rude, so I hugged him, and then turned to hug Shaka, who was standing next to Juan. The Special Activities Coordinator said nothing.

A few weeks later, I got a letter from Shaka.

Dr. Ebony Roberts,

Clenched fist salute sister! May the thoughts of this drumbeat find you and your tribe maintaining the fiery spirit of struggle that was bequeathed to us by our ancestors. As for us here, we are flying high off the positive energy and the possibility of effectuating change.

I am writing at this time to extend a personal thank you for taking the time out of what I imagine to be a hectic schedule to come and share your wisdom with us. Though we have been making some progress in our efforts to liberate the minds of our fellow captives, I believe that you and Rashad's presence have increased our chances tenfold. Most brothers in here have grown accustomed to hearing empty rhetoric, so it was very important to have voices from the outside come in and show them that we can make a change if we are truly committed to the idea of change. It is the first time in a long time that they have witnessed theory being put into practice. I know that it may not seem like much on the surface, but for those of us who overstand the psychological effects of knowing that someone cares, it means a lot.

In extending our thanks I really want to know what else we can do to help you better help us. If we can continue to work from the outside and inside, we will be that much more effective.

I really don't want to hold you too long, so I will close by saying your presence was deeply appreciated and I am personally thankful to you for coming up. We would also like to know when we can expect your return.

Take care and continue to build toward a better tomorrow. I am also enclosing a thank you letter on behalf of those who attended the rites of passage program.

Pamoja tutashinda (Together we will win!)

Shaka

I intended to respond but my life was hectic and his letter got lost in a pile of mail from other inmates.

10

would say I was done with Rashad, write down all the reasons he wasn't good for me, and then loneliness would come and I would call or text him, or he would call me, and I would be back at square one. Like my mama holding on to my daddy, I couldn't let go.

I grew angry with myself. I wanted to be done, but I didn't know how to untangle the yarn that knitted our lives together. We were friends. We were comrades.

One day, kneeling at the edge of my bed, I sobbed, snot dripping, as I begged God to free me. Free me from needing him. Free me from longing for his touch, or any man's touch, so much that I went back to him again and again.

Freedom came through books. Once again, Iyanla's words spoke to me. Her book *Value in the Valley* gave me a lens through which to look at my life. "Everyone comes into our life to mirror back to us some part of ourselves we cannot or will not see. They show us the parts we need to work on or let go." I highlighted what seemed like every other word in the book, making notes in the margins and in my journal. I kept asking myself, What lesson did Rashad come to teach me? What did I need to let go of?

The answers came in moments of solitude. They all led back to my childhood.

On the morning of my thirtieth birthday, I stood in the mirror, staring at my reflection. I thought about the arc of my life: being daddy's little girl, then watching my daddy turn against my mama, my attraction to bad boys and the heartbreak that followed, trying to be the good girl my mama wanted me to be but resenting her for trying to protect me.

The dreadlocs I'd worn for the past seven years suddenly felt heavy. I was ready to cut them and release the energy my hair had been carrying. I grabbed a pair of scissors and without ceremony, started snipping. I cut and I cried as I watched my locs fall to the floor, one by one. I cried for the time I had wasted waiting for Rashad to commit to me. I cried for the times I said I was done and I wasn't. *I can't do this anymore. I can't live like this.* I cut some more. *I surrender. I surrender.*

I wanted a man who would truly love me, who would work alongside me in the community, who would build a family with me, a legacy. But at thirty, with my luck with love, it felt like that would never happen.

I stared in the mirror at my hair, now in a knotty afro, and took a deep breath. "Be patient. Your king is coming," I heard the Creator whisper to me.

I continued my work in prisons and the letters from men on the inside continued to pile up. Sometimes they were looking for help with an appeal or help getting their work published. But then there were the brothers who would lay it on thick. "I need a good woman in my life."

One day I got a letter from Juan, the brother from Carson City. He wanted to build with a conscious sister, he said. Here we go, I thought to myself. I kept reading. He wasn't interested in corresponding with *me*. He wanted me to pass his name and prison number on to a friend, a coworker maybe, who might be interested in writing him.

Juan's letter reminded me that correspondence from the outside keeps the men and women on the inside connected to the free world. To their humanity. I'd only written the men on our mailing list about books or bus rides. I felt guilty for not responding to their letters for help, but I couldn't respond to them all.

I shared Juan's information with my coworker Trina, and then I thought of Shaka. He seemed like a good brother. Maybe I could start with him.

That night I went online. I pulled up OTIS, the Michigan Department of Corrections' offender tracking system, and typed in Shaka's name. A picture half the size of the screen popped up. His face is solemn, his eyes distant. I read his height, weight, birth date, and then scrolled down to read his charges: SECOND DEGREE MURDER. A piece of my heart broke. I didn't know Shaka's story, but I assumed he had gotten caught up in the streets like so many young Black men.

At work the next day, I wrote him a letter.

March 20, 2006
Brother Shaka,

I pray this letter finds you in good health and spirits.
I have been meaning to write you for some time, but I am

so forgetful (despite my youth!). I received a letter the other day from Brother Juan that made me go ahead and write. In his letter, he spoke about the need for conscious female correspondence and asked me to forward his info to some of the sisters I work with. (I work at an African-centered school.) After reading his letter, I thought about you, probably because I met you both at the same time, and wondered if you felt the same. I assume you have sisters you correspond with but may also want to kick it with a sister of like mind.

Terrence gave me your address. I hope that's okay. I've actually never written anyone about anything other than organizational business. While I have received countless letters, most of which I didn't have time to reply to, I am committed to corresponding with you, even if I don't reply right away. I've gotten so used to the fast-paced world of technology that I usually communicate via e-mail or text messaging . . . so I will have to slow down a bit so that I can compose a letter.

I realize how important correspondence with family, friends, and supporters are to our brothers' development; this may ultimately make the difference in the choices they make once they return home. Even still, I've been neglectful in writing. Perhaps because I shoulder much weight as an active member, and now secretary. But I must admit that it helps knowing you are one of Terrence's comrades. That personal connection, although not necessary, makes writing consistently that much easier for someone like me who's very busy and forgetful to boot. I also plan to write Terrence's baba as well.

*Anyway, I am writing you at work, so I must close this
letter. I look forward to building with you.*

In struggle,

Ebony

I signed the letter, put it in an envelope, and then debated
with myself. Do I use my home address or the organization's
address? This wasn't a personal letter, but it also wasn't business. I decided on the latter.

The next week, I got a letter from Shaka. "It would be a
great joy to connect with a sister on a level that goes beyond
the superficial. To me there is no sight as beautiful as an intelligent Black woman who is dedicated to the advancement of
our people. And when you live in a world as consistently ugly
as prison, it is refreshing to have some beauty enter your life."

I smiled.

"When you came up to Carson City, those brothers were
beside themselves having met a sister who understands us.
Most of them had never dealt with a real sister. But I knew
there were sisters like you out there. The way you looked at the
brothers with love and compassion grabbed me. Not only did
I feel like you really understood us, but I knew in the deepest
part of my soul. As you spoke that day you made me think of
Assata Shakur, and after you left, I felt a burning need to connect with you."

I stopped and reread his words: "You made me think of Assata Shakur." I was honored, but something like shame washed
over me. Assata is one of the most revolutionary Black women I
know. In 1973, she was involved in a shootout on the New Jersey Turnpike that led to the death of a white state trooper. She

was charged with first degree murder and, in 1977, convicted by an all-white jury. She was thirty years old. My age. Targeted by the police because of her political activities. Tortured in prison because of her political beliefs. In my mind, I could not possibly live up to her legacy.

"I want to know everything about you," he continued. "Where did you grow up? How did you get involved in the struggle? What is your favorite book? Your favorite food?" The next day, I wrote back. One page turned into eight.

"We are not free," I tell him, prompted by his question about my favorite food. "We are dependent on other people to feed us. The only places to buy groceries in Detroit are the liquor store, the dollar store, or the mostly Arab-owned supermarkets that sell spoiled meats and vegetables and processed foods that have been left on the shelves well past their expiration date. But this is all we have," I explain. "Commercial grocery store chains like Kroger and Farmer Jack have left the city."

I go on to tell him about growing up in Detroit, about As One, about Nsoroma. The words spill onto the page with ease.

Shaka responded to my letter with an equally long letter. "With an impression as deep and lasting as the hieroglyphics on the walls of the great pyramids, your words will forever be etched into my soul," he started. "You are a brilliant writer with a beautiful and fiery spirit that I am drawn to. It really feels good to connect with you on such a profound level and it is very humbling."

He continued the conversation on food that I started in my last letter. "It is no coincidence that we have all of those fast food joints and low-quality grocery stores in our community, but we're focused on the crack dealers and crack houses. If we were to combine every crack house in every ghetto across the country, they would not equal the amount of death and destruction caused by liquor and fast food."

I sat for what seemed like hours, captivated by his words. He understood the movement for our people in the ways I understood. He spoke about the struggle in there and the struggle out here, about sexism in the movement, about his favorite books, about transformation.

He went on in his letter, "This brother gave me *The Autobiography of Malcolm X* and at the time I didn't know anything about Malcolm, so I thought it was some kind of gangster book. But once I started reading it, my whole view of life began to change. As I read about his powerful transformation from a street thug into an uncompromising voice of resistance, I realized the powers that laid dormant within me. When I entered prison, I was a very bitter and angry person and I did not care whether I lived or died. I blamed everyone else for the way my life had turned out. After finishing his book, I wanted to learn more about our history, culture, religion. I became a voracious reader and spent countless hours in the library conducting research. With each book I read, I felt a part of me being redeemed."

I felt an instant connection. I had read *The Autobiography of Malcolm X* in my twelfth-grade English class and was glued to the pages. I didn't know much about Black history then, but Malcolm made me want to know more. He made me want to know the truth. "I began first telling my black brother inmates about the glorious history of the black man—things they never had dreamed," Malcolm wrote. "I told them the horrible slave-trade truths that they never knew. I would watch their faces when I told them that, because the white man had completely erased the slaves' past, a Negro in America can never know his true family name, or even what tribe he was descended from: the Mandingos, the Wolof, the Serer, the Fula, the Fanti, the Ashanti, or others."

Prison has bred many a revolutionary. It is where Malcolm found the Nation of Islam, where George Jackson found Mao and Marxism. "Black Revolutionaries do not drop from the moon," Assata Shakur once wrote. "We are created by our conditions. We are shaped by our oppression. We are being manufactured in droves in the ghetto streets, places like Attica, San Quentin, Bedford Hills, Leavenworth, and Sing Sing. They are turning out thousands of us."

I could easily see Shaka was one of them.

11

The moment I sealed up my letter, a flood of questions came. I started a new one. "How supportive has your family been during your incarceration? What kind of relationship do you have with your father? What skills have you cultivated while in prison? What do you want to do when you return home? What has been the most frustrating aspect of your imprisonment? What has been the ugliest moment? What has been the brightest moment?" I wanted to paint a picture of Shaka, to understand the man he had become.

He answered every question I asked, and some that I didn't, his letter longer than the last one. I was rapt, his words stirring every emotion. He told me about the pain of not being there to raise his two children, about the four and a half years he spent in solitary confinement on 23-hour lockdown, about his mother's absence.

He told me about his mother's rage and how she beat him and his siblings all the time. He told me how he'd grown so tired of the abuse that he ran away, his friends hiding him in their basements for two weeks. He told me how he'd been approached by an older guy, a drug dealer, with an offer he couldn't refuse—$350 a week plus $10 a day for food to sit in a crack house, twenty-four hours a day, seven days a week. He'd have somewhere to lay his head and a way to feed himself. He was fourteen then. I thought of Will and Dre who were about the same age when they started selling drugs.

"I don't really have a relationship with my mother," he wrote. "I have not seen her since 1993 and she only writes every few years or so."

I did not know what to think or say. The pain, the longing is familiar, and I tell him so. "I can relate. When my daddy died, I did not cry." I tell him about the drinking and the arguing. I tell him about the letter I wrote my mama when I was eleven, before my daddy pulled a gun on her, begging her to leave my daddy alone:

> Dear Mother,
>
> I know you still have a little love for daddy, but all he wants to do is come back home and make life miserable for us, but as long as he lives with us and can come and go, anytime that he wants, he's satisfied and happy. He is thinking only of himself. He wants to live with us, but give us nothing, and expect to have dinner ready when he gets home from who knows where. Now, daddy is the type to get lovey-dovey like nothing has happened, and expect everything to be A-OK, and you, feeling sorry for him, fall for his silly little game to come back into our lives,

*but when he gets here, he treats us like dirt and argues
all the time, and half the time, not even home. Daddy
needs to be in a home, I'm serious. He has a problem he
won't admit to. Don't even take him back when he stops
drinking, 'cause you never know when he is going to
turn on you again. I know what you're saying, you can't
hang up when he calls or not even talk to him 'cause he
might take off child support. Look at it this way, we're
not getting anything now anyway, and he's supposed to
be working. Mom, if you take daddy back, it would be a
stupid move! I mean everything I have said in this letter.
Don't let him come in anymore, 'cause one day he might
get mad and hit you or something of that nature. He's evil
and means all harm to us.*

> *Loved always,*
> *Your daughter Ebony*

I tell him about the day I sat in front of my ancestral altar, legs crossed, heart open, and cried for my daddy. I suggested he write his mother and tell her how he felt, wishing I could do the same.

In letters that didn't come soon enough, Shaka and I vibed about family, about religion, capitalism versus socialism, astrology, and community organizing. We need to learn from organizations like the Black Panther Party, he told me. "The Panthers organized around the needs of the people. We need to build from where they left off."

I wrote back. "So many people have romanticized the Black Panther Party and the Black Power Movement. They study the theories the Panthers studied—socialism, communism—but we have to move beyond this sort of cultural romanticism and translate what we've learned from the Panthers and others into something that meets the needs of our people today."

We went on like this for pages. It took longer for Shaka to get my letters than for me to get his—prisoner mail must be inspected, a process that can take three days or longer given the volume of mail most prisons handle in an average week—so that usually meant our conversations were disjointed, his letters always a week behind. But I kept writing. Whenever I wanted to talk to him, I'd start another letter.

"You challenge me," he told me one day. "I have corresponded with others but never has anyone drawn so much out of me or challenged me intellectually the way that you do. You make me want to dig deeper in my commitment to our struggle."

I thought about the letters between Angela Davis and George Jackson, the way Angela opened George's heart, how George inspired Angela's activism.

I thought about how much I enjoyed Shaka's letters, how I never wanted them to end. I thought about how his words made me feel, how they made me think. No man had ever moved me the way Shaka moved me.

He's in prison, I kept reminding myself whenever I finished one of his letters. *He's in prison.*

knew about the clause in the Thirteenth Amendment that permitted slavery *as a punishment for a crime*, but my conversations with Shaka made those words more real.

The best-paying gigs are in the kitchen, he told me. There, an inmate can make as much as 34¢ an hour. This almost-free labor is built into the system, but some states like Alabama and Arkansas and Texas do not pay inmates at all. Their labor is completely free, and their bodies are the property of the state. This is new age slavery.

"I'm not doing no slave labor," Shaka wrote. He'd worked as a baker, a porter, and a law clerk, but there were some jobs he wouldn't do. Jobs that required him to do back-breaking work.

Shaka wanted the young guys in the hood to know about the Thirteenth Amendment and the truth about slavery. To know that they are pawns in a game. To know the streets aren't worth their freedom. He wanted them to choose a different path than he'd chosen. "Our children are being raised by the same system that failed us. That is a frightening thought. It's what drives me to work with at-risk youth." He told me he had written three novels that he believed would inspire the youth he hoped to influence. He called his books conscious street literature.

"The youth of today are enamored with street lit and my books are a way for me to get a message across to a large audience."

"I think you may be on to something. Much of the books published right now about the streets only glamorize that life. That's a great way to reach the youth."

He asked me to help him self-publish his books, and I agreed. Starting his own business meant once he came home, no one could tell him no, you're not qualified, no, you're a murderer. His life would be in his hands.

13

came to crave his words. I craved *him*.

I checked the organization's mail once a week, sometimes more, hoping for a letter from Shaka. When there was, I rushed to my car and opened the envelope as soon as I got inside. His letters were usually typed and no less than three pages long. I'd sit quietly in my car poring over each page, reading and rereading his words again and again.

"You can use my home address," I told him after a month of exchanging letters. It was like switching from snorting cocaine to free-basing—I could get my fix a whole lot faster if the letters came straight to my house. Getting the letters at home brought Shaka further into my life.

One day, while I was sitting on my bed daydreaming, I got lost in the idea of what we could be. Two Black activists working alongside each other, in love, building community, building a family, little brown babies with their tiny Black Power fists raised. I was unsure of the feelings I was feeling but there was something there. I have to tell him, I thought. He must know.

Before I talked myself out of it, I wrote Shaka what I called the love letter that *wasn't* a love letter. It was decidedly *not* a love letter because those feelings weren't there yet, but I wanted him to know how much I was feeling him. A risky step. It felt like free-falling out of an airplane with no parachute.

What will he think? Will he respond? I wondered.

I also wondered whether I was setting myself up to be played. I'd heard the stories about men in prison who manipulated women for money and companionship, making promises to be with them forever. Promises they never planned to keep. Shaka seemed different. Though I didn't really know him, there was something both familiar and fresh about him that made me think my heart would be safe.

I searched my nightstand drawer for the perfect stationery. I settled on a thin, delicate stock with pressed dried flowers. I grabbed my favorite pen and, using my best penmanship, I started writing.

April 30, 2006
Dear Shaka,

As I write this letter, thoughts of you fill my head and warm my heart. Unable to see you or speak to you right now, writing has become my way of reaching out to you. Even though I know it will be a few days before this letter reaches you, I want you to know that I am thinking about you today. I feel a very real connection to you, and it's rare for me to connect with a brother on this level. In each of my letters to you, I find myself wanting to bare my soul, as if you were already a close friend or lover.

The genuineness you sense from me is from the heart. For whatever reason, I feel comfortable being myself and expressing my thoughts to you. I appreciate your openness with me and hope you know I would never betray your trust. When a person opens their heart to you, that's sacred. Most people don't feel safe to share their innermost thoughts or feelings for fear that they will be judged or ridiculed, or their weaknesses exposed. I can't explain it, but I don't care right now if you see this more vulnerable side of me. I want you to know I am imperfect. My life is full of contradictions, many of which I'm cool with. I am a work in progress, and while I hope to leave behind a legacy of power and promise, I am not comfortable with comparisons to Assata Shakur. I want you to get to know the real me, not some image of me you may have created in your head when you first met me. And I want to get to know the real Shaka—your likes, dislikes, your moods, how you treat other people. I know it's hard to really get to know a person under these conditions, but I don't want there to be any illusions. Now you told me you don't play games and I'm holding you to that. And the same goes for me.

While I'm not resisting these feelings, I am cautious. What if I put the time and energy into cultivating our friendship, and then when you come home, you want to plant your garden somewhere else? I hope that I haven't ruined a perfectly good friendship by sharing my feelings.

It is my hope that you feel the same connection with me that I feel with you.

I look forward to reading your thoughts. Until then, know that you have touched a special place in my heart.

Enjoying this connection,

Ebony

Days felt like weeks as I waited for a response to my letter that wasn't a love letter. I rushed home from work every day to check the mail, and nothing. I started overanalyzing. Am I crazy? What if he doesn't feel the same way? What if he *does*?

That week, a couple letters from Shaka arrived, but after reading through what felt like a million pages, I was disappointed to find that neither of them mentioned my letter or the feelings I'd shared. Why hasn't he said anything? Was my letter too much, too soon? Then, finally, those thoughts were quieted when I got *the* letter.

"As I sit here writing this letter, I am imagining what it would feel like to be able to look into your eyes as I shared the contents of my heart. To deny what I feel would be to deny the divine order of things. From the very beginning I have felt a connection to you that was undeniable. I feel honored that you shared your feelings with me. I would never take advantage of your vulnerability."

I devoured the rest of his words. He calmed my fears about being manipulated, about investing my time with no promise of a future. He assured me, "I am at a point in my life where I know not only what I want, but what I need."

I smiled. *A man who seeks what I seek.*

Then, he warned me. "It is very hard to maintain a relationship when one of the partners is in captivity. There will be those moments when you will desire to be held at night and I won't be there to provide the comforting embrace you may need in that moment. There will be times when you may need to vibe with me on a particular issue and the reality of having to wait on the mail to run will kick in. There are those times like right now when I wish that I could just hold your hand and speak the contents of my heart into your ear. There will be so many games played by the state that it will threaten your sanity. Being in a relationship under these conditions will mean that a great deal of responsibility will fall on your shoulders, and though it is only momentary, it may at times seem like forever. I say all of this not as a means to dissuade you, but to ensure that you are as ready as I am to take the first step toward a slow forever."

I wrote him back immediately. "I'm not naïve so I know that it would be a challenge on several levels, but I believe you are worth the investment. I feel a very deep spiritual connection, something I've never felt before. Although we are still learning each other, you have many of the qualities I am attracted to in brothers. I know how rare it is to find someone who you connect with and shares your values and dreams. I have no idea where this friendship will lead but I believe that our meeting was no coincidence. I can only imagine how much closer we will become as we continue to connect through letters and visits. But you should know that I would only make that kind of commitment if we were seriously talking about building a future together. I know there are few promises you can make in this situation."

didn't know why Shaka had gone to prison. I didn't ask. I knew he'd been convicted of second degree murder, and as murders go, that meant he hadn't plotted to kill anybody. Maybe he was in the wrong place at the wrong time. Maybe he was protecting himself. Then one day I got a letter explaining everything.

"It was a hot Saturday night in July 1991," he started. "And that night I was DJing a party. I was selling crack at the time and I had been drinking for most of the day leading up to the party, which was around the corner from where I lived. As the night wore on and the party started to wind down, a couple of the guys from my crew got into it with some other brothers and one of my friends shot one of the brothers, which brought the party to a halt. After everyone left, I packed up the equipment and headed home for the night. It was around two in the morning. When I got home, me and my son's mother were arguing in front of the house when a car slowed down and then parked next door. I had a pistol on me and was on alert because I had been shot on the same block the previous year in a similar fashion, so I was extra cautious. I didn't recognize the car and I knew the guys I was with had just gotten into an altercation. Once the car was parked, the guy in the backseat, who turned out to be one of my regular customers, called me over to the car. When I approached the vehicle, I noticed two white guys in the car who I had never seen before. He asked me to sell him some drugs and I told him I didn't do business like that. I had told him before that I would only deal with him, and to never bring anyone to my house. While he tried to convince me to sell to him, the guy in the passenger seat started talking to me all disrespectful, which made me think he was the police, so I told them to leave. That's when the guy in the passenger seat became even more belligerent. We exchanged some words and I basically told them it would be in their best interest to get off the block. As I turned to walk back to the house, I heard the guy say he would kill me or something like that and when I turned around, he was trying to get out of the car. That's when I started shooting. He was hit four times and died later at the hospital. I will carry the burden of what I did to his family with me forever."

I held the letter in my hand staring at the words. I pictured that night in my head and read the letter again, slowly, to make sure I understood the sequence of events, the characters. I pictured the houses, the trees, the car. I imagined how dark the sky must have been, how quiet the night before gunfire exploded in the still morning air.

I read his words and I thought about the day my daddy could have killed my mama. I thought about Kya, my brother's prom date, and my cousin Lil' Sherman, whose murder seven years earlier devastated my family. The details of Shaka's story didn't change the way I felt about him. He was nineteen then, still hurting from childhood scars. My heart opened more.

15

"Would you be interested in coming up for a visit, so we can speak in person?" Shaka wrote.

I was eager to see if the connection I felt through our letters was real, so I wrote back immediately. "I am definitely interested in coming to visit you. Please add my name to your visitors' list."

I sent in my visiting application and made plans to visit on Saturday, May 20. When the day arrived, I was nervous. The thought of seeing Shaka for the first time since we'd started corresponding overwhelmed me. What if there's no chemistry? What if I'm not attracted to him? What if, what if, what if?

My mind wandered as I drove up I-94 headed to Lakeland Correctional Facility in Coldwater, a prison about two hours north of Detroit. I wondered whether the natural deodorant I was wearing would stand up against the rising heat. It was one of the warmest spring days we'd had and the sweat under my arms was beginning to trickle down my sides. Damn, I should have brought my deodorant, I thought.

When I checked in at the front desk, I was told the prison was in the middle of count, a routine security measure where the officers count all the inmates, bed by bed. This meant that they could not process visits until all inmates were accounted for.

"Have a seat," said the officer behind the desk.

I walked into the lobby and took a seat along the wall. It was after two o'clock and the room was nearly empty. The other visitors, mostly women, sat quietly, their eyes distant. I looked at them sitting alone, the fluorescent lights casting shadows on their pensive faces, and imagined sitting there once a week for the next two years.

The waiting felt like torture. I tried calming my nerves— *You'll be fine. It's just a visit. No pressure*—but none of it worked.

Once count was cleared, an officer started calling up visitors.

"White." No one moved. "White," I heard the name again.

I jumped up. "Here I am," I called. I remembered, Shaka's birth name is White. He'd changed it to an African name after he got to prison.

Any calm I had collected while I waited to be called fled as I walked to the officer. The other women shifted in their seats, their eyes now pointed at me. I clutched the fifteen dollars in quarters I'd stuffed into the shallow pockets of my fitted cotton jacket. *Still there.* The anxiety sat in my chest, each breath a struggle. When I reached the desk, the officer asked for my driver's license, and then escorted me to the first of many security doors I'd have to pass through before I could see Shaka. I stood at the thick Plexiglas door waiting for the officer in the control center to open it. I thought about the moment I'd see Shaka's face and I smiled.

I was brought back to reality when I got a glimpse of myself in the Plexiglas. I started to panic. Months earlier, I had started letting my short natural hair grow and it was in an awkward in-between phase. I didn't look like I did that day in Carson City when we first met. My long locs were now gone. I had decided to wear a headwrap to match my outfit, like I often did, but I was starting to question that decision. I didn't know the prison's dress code. What if headwraps weren't allowed and they made me remove it?

Just as that realization hit me, the officer asked about the headwrap.

"I wear it for religious reasons," I lied.

"Okay, but we're gonna have to inspect it," he warned me.

"That's fine," I responded coolly, then sighed. I had no Plan B—no comb, no brush, nothing, and by then my short afro was patted down and uneven.

The officer didn't say anything about the rest of my outfit but I later discovered that my fitted cotton jacket and the white tank top that didn't entirely conceal my bra could have gotten my visit terminated if I had come earlier or later, or another day altogether. Sometimes what is allowed depends on the officer's mood.

"Inappropriate" clothing is the number one reason visitors get denied. Rules for women are much more strict than they are for men. A woman's pants can't be too tight and her jeans can't have any holes. Her skirt can't be too short, and if there's a split in the back or front, it can't come above the knee. And shirts are tricky. Shirts can't be cut too low in the front or the back, or expose her belly or her bra strap, even slightly. That day, I got lucky.

Once the security door opened, I stepped inside a small room with a metal detector, a table, and a few chairs. I put the quarters and my license in a basket on the table and walked through the metal detector. A female officer waited on the other side ready to pat me down. With my arms raised shoulder height, she moved her hands along the silhouette of my body, checking my front and back pockets and underneath my breasts. She then instructed me to take off my shoes and socks and lift my feet. When I was done putting my shoes and socks back on, she asked me to stand and patted my head lightly.

"Step over here," she said. "I'm going to need to check the inside of your headwrap."

Hidden from the male officers, I unwrapped the long African fabric that hid my uneven afro so the officer could inspect underneath for contraband, and then quickly rewrapped the fabric.

I had wrapped my crown a thousand times before, but usually in front of a mirror, making sure the fabric laid perfectly. This time, all I had was the security mirror that hung from the ceiling ten feet above my head. I took a quick look in the mirror when I was done, and as far as I could tell, I didn't look crazy. I was then escorted through another Plexiglas door and waited in a short hallway for the door to the visiting room to be opened.

I closed my eyes and took a deep breath.

The door opened slowly as if another dimension had been

unlocked. I walked into the room, my heart pounding, my armpits still sweating, and stopped. I noticed a row of inmates in their blue and orange uniforms seated to my right and tried to find Shaka's face. I stood there for what seemed like forever, feeling awkward and insecure like the new kid waiting to be picked for kickball. Finally, our eyes met. Shaka stood up and walked quietly toward me. The anxiety in my chest made its way up my throat and stayed there. He greeted me with a half-smile, his face still as serious as I remembered, and then he hugged me, his big broad chest swallowing my small frame. I said something, maybe hello, but I'm not sure.

Shaka looked nothing like I remembered him—he wore a pair of state-issued glasses that were unflattering, and his dreadlocs hung like a wet mop instead of the regal mane I'd remembered—but when he grabbed my hand, his hand felt like home. Our fingers fit together perfectly as if two misplaced puzzle pieces had found each other.

The room was Spartan-like with nothing but thirty or so hard plastic chairs, two vending machines, and a podium, which served as a perch for the officer whose job was to make sure no one touched inappropriately or passed contraband. Shaka led me to a set of seats in the middle of the room and we sat down. We weren't allowed to move the chairs, so we sat side-by-side, twisting our heads and then our bodies so we could look at each other as we talked.

We broke the ice with small talk about my drive up, then picked up where we'd left off in our letters. The way we eased in and out of conversation made whatever nerves I still had melt away.

"I'm really feeling the preschool," Shaka told me. "I'm willing to do whatever I can to help you make it a reality. I could do most, if not all, of the research you need on African culture, geography, spiritual systems, economic systems."

"That would be dope. Thank you. The curriculum has to be tight, you know. I got to bring the best to the babies."

"Indeed. Our children deserve nothing but the best. Our conditions demand it."

We were so enthralled in our conversation that it was a few hours into our visit before I remembered the quarters I had in my pocket. "I'm so sorry, I forgot I had these quarters," I interrupted.

Shaka laughed. "It's okay, I'm not really hungry."

"Are you thirsty?" I asked.

I walked to the vending machines and rattled off the options to Shaka. Michigan inmates aren't allowed to handle money or walk around the visiting room, so he eyeballed the vending machine from our seats and told me what he wanted. I bought a bag of chips and a soda for him and chips and a water for me.

We scarfed down the chips as we talked. It was an unusual place for a first date, but halfway into our visit I forgot where we were. In between mouthfuls, Shaka told me, "I've never felt as connected to anyone as I do to you in this moment." I felt the same.

We spent the rest of the day lost in conversation, and three hours later, the officer called out, "Visiting hours are now over." Everyone in the room stood to say their goodbyes. Shaka and I hugged. He wrapped his arms around me as far as they would reach, and I leaned into his hard, muscular frame. We lingered for a moment. No words were spoken.

When our faces parted, he reached down to kiss me. I hesitated. I didn't know we'd be able to kiss. He pecked me on the lips and then opened his mouth. I closed my eyes and welcomed his tongue. We kissed awkwardly for a couple minutes, starting and stopping. I couldn't focus. All I could think about was the bag of Fritos I'd gotten from the vending machine, the taste still in my mouth, and the officer's vigilant eyes, clocking the movement of our tongues, our hands.

"Time to go," the officer called, stopping us the moment we found our rhythm.

We pulled apart and our eyes met. I wanted more.

I smiled all the way to the car and on the drive back to Detroit. I'd started the visit nervous and unsure about what I was feeling, but by the end, as I felt my heart, my body come alive, I knew we were meant to be.

16

D ays later Shaka was transferred to Cooper Street Correctional Facility in Jackson. We had mixed feelings. He'd been moved closer, an hour from Detroit instead of two, and that meant I'd be able to visit more often, but there was a possibility he could be transferred farther away to a prison camp in northern Michigan. Cooper Street is a transitional facility where guys go before they are sent home or elsewhere in the system, usually a camp.

Shaka was allowed eight visits a month and I visited every weekend, sometimes more. He could be transferred any day, so we enjoyed each moment we had together. No matter how full the room, it always felt as if we were alone. Sometimes we sat, the two of us, in silence, listening to the clamor of voices around us. I would lean against him, trying to close whatever space was between us, and we'd watch the other people in the room—the children playing on laps, the women doting on the men, the men smiling their first real smiles of the day.

We took a picture every visit. Pictures were $3 and we were allowed to kiss and hug again. Those moments were the highlight of our visit, but one Saturday, we didn't take a picture. That day when I signed in, the officer at the front desk told me I couldn't wear my headwrap, which I'd been wearing every visit since our first one at Lakeland.

"I wear it for religious reasons."

"Do you have a letter from your religious leader?"

I stared at her. I didn't have a letter. I didn't even have a religious leader. "No, but I haven't had any problems before," I told her, hoping that was enough to get me by another day.

"Well, ma'am, that's the policy."

"But no one has ever asked me for a letter and I've been visiting here for almost a month," I continued, now feeling this was personal.

"I don't know what to tell you, ma'am, but you can't wear that today," she said with finality.

I faked a smile and walked away from the desk, trying not to show the panic in my face. I still didn't have a backup plan—no comb, no brush, not even a headband—but I had traveled an hour to see Shaka so I wasn't about to turn around and go home. I went into the restroom, unwrapped the fabric from my head, and looked at my uncombed afro. I took a deep breath, patted my hair, and returned to the lobby that was now full with expectant visitors. I put the fabric in a locker with my purse and walked back to the desk. The officer had a look of satisfaction on her face. I wanted to say "Fuck you," but I didn't. I knew officers like her, white people like her who antagonized Black people just because they could. I refused to give her more power.

On almost every visit, we'd sit and reminisce about growing up in Detroit in the eighties—the decline of the auto industry, white flight, Mayor Coleman Young, the rise of crack cocaine, the golden era of hip-hop, riverfront festivals, Belle Isle.

"You remember the Giant Slide?"

"Man, we used to go down to Belle Isle every summer. We'd roll deep to the Giant Slide. Them stairs were no joke though!"

"I know, right? But we'd go up and down them stairs all day, thighs burning."

We laughed.

I told Shaka about my family's summer trips to Mississippi and he told me about nights in front of the fireplace at his family's east side home, when his parents were still together. We talked about the good times we had as children, and we talked about the bad. What we did not share in our letters, we bared on our visits.

He told me about the time, after he'd run away from home and started selling drugs, he was beaten and left for dead in a crack house. He told me about his struggle with addiction and the demons he'd fought. He told me about the things he'd seen and the things he'd done trying to survive in the streets. "When I look back on those times, it is like looking at a whole different person. I can no longer identify with the nigga I had become. Those were some dark days. I didn't care whether I lived or died."

Once I started opening up, I didn't stop. I told Shaka about the times that the tension in our house was thick, almost suffocating—the body language, the silence, my mama's contempt for my daddy palpable. I told him about the night Daddy walked away with bloody scratches and a handful of Mama's hair while I watched a few feet away. I told him how I tried to stay out of their way when they fought.

When I told him about what happened in that basement bathroom, his heart broke right before my eyes. "I'm so sorry that happened to you," he said, caressing the back of my hand.

I'm not sure I was molested, I told him. I don't remember what happened next. Maybe I wasn't molested, I questioned myself. He had to touch me, right? I had to be violated more than once, right? Maybe I blocked the other incidents out like I'd blocked out what happened after he pulled out his penis. I tried to remember more. I couldn't. But what I do remember I will never forget.

Shaka assured me, "You were molested, Ebony." By then, I'd told a handful of people, family, about what happened. It was my secret. I was protecting the man who had taken my innocence as much as I was protecting myself. I had been wearing a mask, pretending to others I was okay. But with Shaka, I showed myself, all the parts I had hidden.

I told him about the things I'd done with my neighbor, a girl, something I'd never told anyone. She was two years older than me and already had breasts and when she made my nine-year-old body feel things it had never felt before, I didn't stop her. When she instructed me to do those same things to her, I did exactly as she told me. I wanted her to be my best friend.

Shaka didn't judge me. Instead he helped me unpack the feelings I had been too afraid to explore out loud.

"I questioned my sexuality for years. I love men, Black men, but I thought maybe I could be bi because I liked it. I knew it was wrong to like it so I didn't tell my mother, or my brother. I didn't think they'd understand."

"First, what happened to you should have never happened. That doesn't mean you're gay, or bi. You were a child."

I gave a voice to the little girl who'd been confused. I felt free. Free from the shame, from the guilt. Mama had told me not to tell a man everything. "Keep some things to yourself or they'll throw it back in your face," she warned me. But it felt good to be vulnerable, to have no secrets.

17

One day, at the end of our visit, something was differ- ent when Shaka and I kissed. He was not there with me. He didn't kiss me with the same abandon, not caring where we were.

"What's wrong," I asked, concerned. "Is it me?"

"No, it's not you."

He didn't have an answer for me then, but later he wrote me. "There is something I wish I had shared with you before you came to visit me that first time. But I will share it with you now because I need for you to understand every part of who I am and what I feel like being in here. When we share moments of intimacy, I am always conscious that we are being watched and scrutinized by the enemies of love. Being in this place, I have grown accustomed to having every aspect of my life placed under scrutiny. Everywhere I turn I am being watched, analyzed, and probed by the eyes of guards and captives. There are very few moments when I can just be. But your presence in my life is changing that. When I am engaged in a conversation with you, no matter how full the room, I feel as though we are alone in our own sacred space. Any hesitancy you may have felt was not a reflection of my lack of desire to hug and kiss you. I love how your lips feel against mine, but I am learning to just be when in your presence. Please be patient with me."

I, too, was still learning to just be. Each visit, I tried to forget where we were, forget that we were being watched. When we kissed, I blocked out the couples around us, also kissing. I closed my eyes and went somewhere else in my mind, a happy place, a place where we were alone, and free. If I didn't, I was distracted. That moment, that kiss was all I had so I savored it. I recorded every move of his tongue, the softness of his lips, the placement of his hands on my waist, just above my hips, so I could remember later, when he wasn't there to hold me or kiss me.

18

t was as if Shaka knew every word in the English language. He'd drop words like *effulgent* or *grandiloquent* or *laconic* in his letters as though they were a part of his everyday vocabulary. One day I joked, "You sound like Oswald Bates," the character played by Damon Wayans in the sketch comedy *In Living Color*. He laughed.

I loved that Shaka was well-read. He expanded my vocabulary and took me with him to the places in his mind. When I missed his words, I'd reread his letters while I waited for the mailman to deliver more.

Eventually we started weekly phone calls, on Sundays. We talked for what seemed like hours, flirting and cracking jokes, our laughter lingering in the air. "Hearing you laugh does wonders for my soul," he wrote to me between our Sunday calls.

One call was only fifteen minutes. It was never enough, but for those fifteen minutes I would forget where he was and we'd kick it on the phone like any other couple.

"Hey, baby!" I'd answer, excited to hear his voice.

"Hello, gorgeous, how are you?"

He'd listen to me ramble on about my day for the first minutes of our call and then I'd ask him about his day.

"Good. I worked out, responded to a couple letters, chopped it up with one of my guys." No matter how monotonous his days were, he'd answer my question as if every day was different, and I'd listen as if something new and exciting had happened. It felt good to talk without a pair of eyes watching us.

I was always jarred back to reality when the operator said, "You have one minute." Sometimes I'd tell Shaka, "Call me back." I wasn't ready to say goodbye.

"Are you sure?" he'd ask. "I don't want the phone bill to be too high." One call was $7.82 and calls added up quickly if we weren't paying attention. He'd always give in and call me one more time.

Shaka was the first to say *I love you.* "I have been thinking of you all day and night," his letter started. "I thought I would share with you what is in my heart. I know I was given the greatest gift by the Creator and the ancestors when you were brought into my life. When I lie awake at night, I think of how much we have shared and how much it feels like I have grown. For years I was apprehensive about opening up to people because I was tired of being hurt and betrayed. I never wanted to feel like that again. But one morning I woke up and went to conduct a program for the brothers and I met you. From that first moment, I wanted you. I wanted your soul to be forever connected to mine. And I have loved you ever since. You have grown to mean more to me than I could have ever imagined." I pictured him there with me looking into my eyes as he professed his love. I knew I loved him too. "I want you to know that you are not under any pressure to move faster than you are ready to," he continued. "We will take things one step at a time."

On our next visit, I told him I loved him. "I see beyond the crime you were convicted of. I see more than your prison number. I see a beautiful soul. My world has become a brighter place since you entered it. You are a blessing."

I saw the weight of prison leave his shoulders. "Knowing that you are willing to look beyond the bars and fences into my heart and soul means the world to me."

When it was time to say our goodbyes, we held each other and kissed like we always did, but this time it felt as if our bodies had fallen away and our souls were kissing. It was unlike anything I'd ever experienced. We were transported out of that room and into another space, another time. Our tongues danced and got lost in a rhythm all their own, a dance we had not rehearsed, wild and free.

Days later, I got a letter from Shaka. He called the kiss magical. "The love we have is deeper than a superficial emotional longing," he wrote. "What we have is a spiritual connection guided by the ancestors. It is a love of the deepest part of who we are. A love that reaches into all of those sacred spaces."

For the first time in my life, I felt safe. I wrote Shaka:

infinite possibilities

you mean the world to me
my life, sweeter

my love, deeper
    growing with each moment we share
    each kiss, caress, touch, word, look, laugh
ever since you smiled at me with your words
your letters like sunrays giving me warmth and light
i have known the greatest joy
my spirit be at peace
    whenever, wherever i think of you
never knew love could feel this good
be so complete
    no assembly required
our love, it knows no boundaries
just infinite possibilities

19

was the one to initiate our first conversation about sex.

"My feelings for you are becoming more and more intense and I know if you were out here, it would be hard for me to keep my clothes on," I wrote.

"Now you know you ain't right for dropping that image on me. I can only imagine that it would be quite hard for both of us to remain clothed considering the depth of our spiritual, intellectual, and emotional connection."

This evolved into a discussion about what turned us on and what we enjoyed sexually. "How do you like to be touched?" Shaka asked. He listened with his heart, not his manhood. "When you have a connection like the one we share, a kiss becomes more than a kiss, a touch more than a touch. Lovemaking becomes something divine. I want to worship your body. I want to kiss you from the crown of your head to the soles of your feet, leaving a trail of fire on every area in between."

I'd never been touched tenderly, with love. His words stirred my imagination. I thought of what our first time together would be like. I thought of his soft lips on my skin. Suddenly two years seemed like a lifetime. Would I be able to wait?

"Would you be okay if I got my sexual needs met by some-one else?" I asked Shaka one afternoon.

"The short answer is hell no," he replied, chuckling.

Shaka was the philosopher. He'd read Plato and Cheikh Anta Diop and studied the Tao Te Ching. There was never a short answer with him.

I smiled, "What's the long answer?"

"Each partner in a relationship has to be willing to make whatever sacrifices are needed to make the relationship work. And I'd like to think that I am a brother who is worthy of a woman making that kind of sacrifice. I am mindful that it isn't the easiest of sacrifices to be made but it really comes down to self-mastery and self-control. When you look at the Sphinx, it is a tremendous example of craftsmanship. The long, majestic body of the lion adorned with the head of a great Pharaoh. The Sphinx, in its wisdom, tells the greatest story of our potential. I interpret the human head sitting on top of the beastly body to mean that the body, or our sexual desires, must be ruled by the head or the mind. It is the natural order of things."

"That's deep. I've never looked at the Sphinx that way."

"Yeah, it's deep. My line of thinking is that I will hold my queen to the same standards or expectations that I hold myself to, and I would want her to hold me to the same standards she has for herself. I know my self-worth as a man and I feel that I am worth waiting for."

"Honestly, I cannot imagine being with someone else. Even

if you said you were okay with that, I couldn't do it. I want to save myself for you."

"To know that my queen is willing to wait until I come home means a great deal to me. It says to me that our connection is deeper than casual sex and that you have the strength to endure hardship. It is our responsibility to put forth an effort to meet each other's needs as best we can under the circumstances."

We talked about what that would look like. Phone sex. Suggestive pictures. Erotic letters. Our sexual thoughts first showed up in between the mushy stuff and then became full scenes detailing what we wanted to do to each other. "Imagine this," I wrote. "You're sitting in the bed reading a book and I'm in the kitchen cleaning up the dishes from dinner when you hear the faint sound of music coming from the living room. Before you can get up to see what's going on, I enter the bedroom. 'Wassup?' you say. 'You,' I respond as I begin to undress to the sounds of Maxwell's 'Til the Cops Come Knockin.' Your eyes catch a glimpse of my nipple and you smile quietly as you slide back in the bed. I continue to dance, swaying my hips to the beat of the music. As I approach the bed, you sit up straight in anticipation of my next movement. I reach over and kiss you softly as I grab your face, bringing you closer to me. I kiss my way down your neck and then your chest . . ."

Shaka matched my passion. His stories rivaled the hottest erotic novels. He'd go on and on, sometimes for three pages or more. I couldn't wait to re-create the pictures we painted with our words.

20

No one knew I had been traveling back and forth to Cooper Street every week. Anything could happen, I thought. I should tell somebody when I'm on the road.

I wasn't looking forward to telling my mama, but she was the person I always called when I was headed out of town. I could count on a prayer before I left, and a "Praise God" when I got to my destination. The day I mustered the courage, Mama and I had just come from a cousin's wedding. A beautiful ceremony in a historic church with breathtaking European architecture. It was a clear blue afternoon in June, the perfect day for a wedding. The sanctuary was full of family, my cousin the third of my aunt's six daughters to get married. She was madly in love. And he was too. It was in their eyes, the way they looked at each other throughout the day. I took it all in, thinking of me and Shaka, of our unexpected love story. I knew he was the man I wanted to spend the rest of my life with. I dreamt of a small wedding by the water with family and close friends, exchanging vows in a traditional African ceremony. *One day, that will be us.*

I didn't know where to start or what to say so I stalled for nearly an hour, sitting in my mama's living room chatting about the wedding and the family, waiting for the perfect moment. But how do you ease into *that* conversation? You don't. You just go for it. I knew Mama would have all kinds of fits no matter what I said, or how I said it. So I started, "Ma, I've been writing this guy in prison . . ."

She heard me out, her eyes locked on me as I told her how Shaka and I met and how much he meant to me. "What's he in prison for?" she asked dryly, still staring. When I told her second degree murder, her face fell and her shoulders collapsed from the weight of all her fears, her hopes of me marrying a "good guy" gone. She had done everything to keep me out of the streets, from the danger that followed dating dope dealers and "thugs."

"You're a fool," she replied, her eyes mixed with disappointment and worry.

I didn't respond. I expected as much.

"I hope he doesn't come home and murder you," she continued.

Her words echoed in my mind. *I hope he doesn't come home and murder you . . . murder you . . . murder you.*

We sat there in awkward silence. I felt like I was fifteen again and she was sitting in not-so-silent judgment of my dating choices.

I had nothing left to say and she was either too hurt or too angry to say anything more, so after a full minute of silence, I left.

I wanted to tell her I didn't care what she thought. I wanted to say Shaka wasn't anything like my daddy. He wasn't going to hurt me. I wanted to tell her how brilliant he was, how he made me feel, how my heart fluttered when I read his letters. But I didn't say any of that.

I felt misunderstood. I felt alone. She hadn't *tried* to understand my love for Shaka, as my mother, as a woman who had been in love. I wondered about the things she'd taught me as a Christian—compassion, brotherly love, redemption. Where was her compassion?

Alone in my house that night, I thought about the pain she'd endured throughout her eighteen-year marriage to my daddy. She'd talked to me about their problems but I know there was still a lot I didn't know. She wanted more for me. "I don't want to see you go through what I went through," she'd tell me. Men weren't to be trusted. They weren't to be depended on to pay the bills, to help with the kids, to love you.

I ignored her warnings.

My reassurances that Shaka was different, that he was a good man, a man who had grown and changed, fell on deaf ears. For Mama, he was in prison. Period.

I had cousins who'd gone to prison, or did short stints in jail, but we never talked about them. We were good, hardworking people with Christian values. We didn't lie. We didn't steal. We didn't hurt people. That was the life they chose. And they got no sympathy from Mama.

I never saw my mother with another man after Daddy died. I did not see her in love or be loved. That is not to say she didn't date, but she had given up on love. It pained me to know my

daddy had hurt her so deeply, that she was so cynical about relationships, but I kept telling myself, that's her story, not mine.

I wanted Mama's blessing, but I'd have to be okay without it.

The next day, I drove up to Cooper Street. I was excited to see
Shaka, but I wasn't looking forward to telling him about the
conversation I'd had with my mama. I didn't want to hurt him
and I knew her words would sting. About an hour into our visit,
once we'd settled in, I started, "I talked to my mama . . ."

"Wow, baby. Thank you," he whispered. "It means the world
to me that you shared our relationship with your mother. I know
that wasn't easy. It feels good to know I'm not a secret, that you
love and respect me enough to tell the woman who gave birth
to you about our relationship. What did she say?" He paused,
his eyes hopeful.

I didn't have the courage to tell Shaka *everything* Mama
said. "Eh, she was disappointed."

I tried to move on, but he could tell I was holding back.
"What did she say? I can take it," he assured me.

I wanted to tell him, but I couldn't bring myself to say the
words. I could not bear to hear them again, not even from my
own mouth.

"Maybe I can write her a letter. Do you think that will help?"

"It couldn't hurt."

I gave Shaka my mama's address. He put a letter in the mail
that week. He told her why he'd turned to the streets, about the
night he'd taken a man's life, about his transformation. He was
open and honest, like he was with me.

"I am not the same young man who walked through the prison doors full of anger, bitterness, and hurt. Today I stand as an example of the human spirit's ability to change. I am proud of the man I am today. There is no expectation for you to change your view or how you feel about me and Ebony. All I ask is that you take the time to get to know me and judge me based on what you find. I want you to know you have a tremendous daughter with an amazing spirit. When we first met, I felt an immediate connection to her and I feel blessed having her in my life. She is the first person I have ever been able to connect with on a deep intellectual, emotional, and spiritual level and she is the only person who I feel really gets me. She inspires me to reach the heights of my human potential. I cherish the friendship we have, and I am looking forward to continuing this journey with her."

I hoped Shaka's letter would make a good impression on my mama and she would see he wasn't in fact a coldhearted killer. I wanted her to see what I saw. But nothing he said changed how she felt—he was still in prison and still convicted of murder.

"I believe that in her own time she will come to see me for who I am and at that point she will know you have made a wise decision," Shaka tried to comfort me.

I hope so, I whispered to myself, the image of us on a June day getting married like my cousin, surrounded by family, fixed in my mind.

didn't look like the women men in prison dream about, the fantasy girl, the one in hip-hop magazines with the toned body and ample derriere. *Would I be enough?*

I kept thinking of the day Rashad studied me as I stood naked in front of his mirror. How I felt that day and every day thereafter whenever I looked at myself in a full-length mirror. The rejection sat in my bones. I thought of Shaka's first day home, him discovering my dimpled flesh, critiquing me like Rashad had, and deciding he didn't want me.

I know him better than this, I kept telling myself. Shaka loves me. He's not shallow. But I had to be sure. *I have to tell him.*

"I have cellulite." I told Shaka about the things Rashad said to me. I told him how his words made me feel. "I'm still healing," I warned.

"I'm a patient brother," he assured me.

Later, on a visit, when Shaka touched me on the back of my arm, I cringed, waiting for him to say something about how flabby my arm was. He noticed me tense up.

"What's wrong?"

"My arms. They're flabby, I know."

"There's nothing wrong with your arms. You've got arms like a woman," he said, his words disarming me. "Baby, it's okay, I'm here now. Fuck him."

"I know, but ten compliments can't undo the damage of one hurtful comment overnight," I explained.

"A lot of people don't understand how damaging verbal abuse can be, but I do. My mother was very abusive physically and verbally and I never felt like I was good enough. I know my compliments won't erase the pain, but I need you to know you are perfect to me."

I blushed, my eyes begging for more.

"I need you to understand you are dealing with a man unlike any you have ever encountered. I want you to allow me to love you the way you need and deserve. I don't want you to feel pressured to live up to some fantasy girl you've concocted in your mind and I don't want you to feel insecure about something as superficial as a little cellulite. That cellulite and your not-so-flat stomach tell me that you are a real woman, which is what my fantasy girl is, not some Hollywood interpretation of beauty."

In the weeks that followed, between visits and letters, we peeled back more layers. One day I wrote him, "I've thought I was in love many times, but I've never felt like the brother was really into me like I was into him. When it came to sex, there was no romance, just a release. When I think of the term 'make love,' I think of a sensual experience between two people who are in love with each other. Fucking is all about the physical connection, and the brothers I've dealt with only referred to sex as fucking. I wouldn't dare say we were making love, afraid that they might think I was too emotional or reading too much into the relationship. Who wants to be the one all into the sex on an emotional level and the other person isn't? So I disconnected my emotions from the act of sex. It was like I put up a wall, so I wouldn't be hurt. I tried to convince myself that I didn't need 'all of that.' " I thought about how I had given my virginity away to a boy I didn't even like just so I wouldn't feel anything for Dre, the boy I thought I loved. I cried as I typed, the memories flooding my head. I had sought from men what they could not give me—love.

Shaka's poetic words spoke to the twelve-year-old girl who wanted a boy to be crazy about her. I was beautiful. I was smart. I was worthy. In his eyes, I deserved the world. Shaka's love buried years of heartache and longing. I knew I couldn't ever let him go.

Week after week, Shaka eased whatever fears I had with the sheer will of his words. He knew what he wanted, and it was me. I enjoyed the attention. His promises to spoil me and show me how much he appreciated me made me love him even more.

"Thank you for loving me for who I am," I wrote him. "This is the first time I've truly felt like a brother loved me unconditionally, from the soles of my feet to the crown of my head. What we have is a very beautiful thing and I just have to keep reminding myself that you are a different kind of brother."

22

didn't have to wait. I didn't have to write or take his calls or send money or travel up and down the highway every week. I'd *chosen* this life. And in choosing, I had to accept that Shaka's life was at the mercy of the Department of Corrections. That meant he could be moved without warning.

Shaka had been at Cooper Street for about a month when I got the call. I picked up after the first ring.

"Hey, baby!"

"Hello, gorgeous," he replied, without his usual lilt. I knew immediately something was up.

"What's wrong?"

"They're transferring me to a camp upstate," he explained. He was being moved to one of the nine prisons scattered across the Upper Peninsula. I wouldn't find out which one until he got there. Our weekly visits were coming to an end.

"Baby, nooo," I cried, my voice starting to crack. "I was looking forward to spending your birthday with you tomorrow." Celebrating birthdays, or love, in a place that tries to kill whatever joy one might find is an act of resistance, however small, and Shaka had never celebrated his birthday. I didn't want them to win.

"I know, gorgeous. It's okay, you've already made my birthday special," Shaka tried to comfort me. "Just having you in my life has been the greatest gift."

"I was planning to surprise you with a special birthday song." It was a song we sang at Nsoroma whenever there was a birthday.

"You can still sing it to me."

"Okay, but I don't know how to sing so you better not laugh," I joked, breaking the tension. I cleared my throat. "Kuziliwa kwa furaha to you, I love you so much, I love you I do. Kuziliwa kwa furaha from the nation to you, all the ancestors send their blessings to you. The seasons are changing for you and for me, as we struggle to be strong, African, free! Kuziliwa kwa furaha to you, I love you so much, I love you I do."

There was silence, and then he spoke. "Wow, thank you, baby. That was beautiful."

We continued talking for whatever minutes remained on that 15-minute call and then he called back a couple more times before we said goodnight. I cried as we talked about the time we spent getting to know each other and how much we were going to miss our weekly visits. That time had been a gift. We grew closer than we thought possible. Our bond had been cemented, and now the distance would test the foundation we'd built.

I knew couples who had grown apart under the pressure of

long distance, and with the added pressure of prison, I knew the odds that we'd survive were slim. But I wasn't a quitter. I had prayed for a man *just like him*. I couldn't just walk away.

I wrote Shaka.

> *i have waited a lifetime for a brother like you to come into*
>   *my life*
> *longed for you*
> *dreamt about you*
> *and me*
> *and the future We would build together*
> *the children We would raise*
>   *little scholars,*
>   *warriors in training*
>   *following in our footsteps, as We have followed in*
>   *those who came before us*
>
> *the Creator has been preparing me for a brother like you*
>   *to share my life*
> *to love, to nurture*
> *to listen, to understand*
> *to struggle together*
>   *and then struggle some more*
>   *knowing i got his back and he got mine, and*
>   *together*
>   *with the spirit of the ancestors as our guide and*
>   *inspiration*
>   *there is nothing We cannot do*
>
> *yes, i have been waiting on you patiently*
> *knowing that you were waiting for me*

to help shoulder the weight
to be your strength when you are weak
to comfort you
and treasure you
to build a slow forever

no, i am not afraid
to put in some work
you no, We
     are worth the long drives, the ritual searches, the
          collect calls, the rising postage, the lonely nights

no, i am not afraid
because I have been waiting a lifetime for you

Days after Shaka's transfer to a prison camp in Manistique, he was moved once more, this time to Baraga Maximum Correctional Facility, a prison on the northern border of the Upper Peninsula.

"The ride up here was crazy," he tells me in a letter once he gets settled. "We stopped at three other prisons before they finally dropped me off. We were on the bus from around 10:30am to about 6:00pm. The only good thing was they gave me my property as soon as I got here so I didn't have to wait until the next day. The bad thing was the shower was closed due to a maintenance problem, so I had to take a bird bath until this morning. I haven't spoken to any of the counselors yet, so I am unsure how long I will be here. But from what I hear, they like to keep guys here for at least six months to a year. If that turns out to be the case, we will just have to ride it out. The good thing is, after that period I will be able to get back down state."

Baraga is eight hours from Detroit, most of the drive through the rural back roads of northern Michigan. I didn't want to make that drive alone. That meant just letters and phone calls for a while.

Time became my enemy, punishing me for loving Shaka. Two weeks felt like two months and all I could think of was the next time I'd get to see him and touch him and smell him. "Baby, no matter how hard it gets, you have to know that our love can survive this," Shaka tried to comfort me. But my heart was grieving.

One day my coworker Trina, the one who'd agreed to write Juan, told me she had started corresponding with an old friend who was in prison, a guy she went to high school with. I told her about Shaka. I told her how we met and how dope our connection was. I told her how much I missed him.

"Are you going to wait for him?"

"Yeah. That's my baby."

"Where is he?" she asked.

"He's in Baraga. That's in the U.P."

"For real? That's where my friend is."

"Are you kidding? What a coincidence. I wonder if they know each other."

She told me more about their story, and I shared more of ours. She told me she would ride with me to Baraga and I couldn't contain my excitement. Then she told me she wasn't on her friend's visiting list.

"I don't have to visit him. I can just hang out at the hotel."

"Girl, no. Write him and tell him to put you on his list."

She hesitated.

"What's up?"

"I haven't seen him in ten years."

"So you don't want to see him?"

"I do, but I don't know if he wants to see me. I'll write him tonight."

"Whatever happens, I'll pay for everything and do all the driving, all you have to do is be the deejay."

"Are you sure? I can give you something on the gas and the hotel."

"I'm sure. I'm just happy to have the company."

"Well how about I pack us some sandwiches or something for the trip? I wouldn't feel right if I didn't contribute something."

I immediately started making plans. I wanted Shaka and I to be able to spend as much time together as possible, and since Nsoroma was on summer break, I planned a five-day trip. I couldn't wait to tell Shaka.

That week, Trina's friend wrote her back and added her to his list. I drove up to Ryan Correctional Facility, one of two medium-security prisons in Detroit, and picked up a visiting application for her. She filled it out right away and mailed it to the facility. Two weeks later, she called me with good news—she'd been approved.

Shaka and I started counting down the days.

I couldn't sleep the night before our trip. We agreed to leave early in the morning so we could make visiting hours that day, and since Trina lived on the east side of the city near I-75, the highway that would take us up north, I stayed the night with her.

The sky was coal black when we packed up the car for the long trip. Trina had bought snacks and made sandwiches, as promised, but we needed to get ice for the cooler. "We can stop around the corner at the gas station," she told me.

I locked the car doors as soon as Trina got out to get the ice. I didn't play when it came to locking doors or pumping gas or walking into the house at night. Mama would always tell my brother and me, whenever we got in the car to go anywhere, or got out of the car, "Lock the door." Always be aware of your surroundings, she'd say. I looked in my rearview mirrors and didn't see any movement. Then suddenly, a man appeared out of the darkness, his eyes deep in their sockets, his brown skin ashen, and his clothes disheveled. I wished Trina would hurry up. I looked away when he noticed me looking at him, and then looked again, keeping my eye on him as he crossed the front of my car. I shifted in my seat. What is taking her so long, I whispered to myself. Seconds later, Trina reappeared. I unlocked the doors. I saw her notice the man as she hopped back in the car. "All right, let's go. I can put the ice in the cooler once we get on the road," she said.

Trina was easy to talk to. We laughed and reminisced and got to know each other outside of work.

"Are you nervous?"

"Girl, yes." Trina had never visited anyone in prison and she told me things between her and her friend had gotten more serious.

"I remember my first visit with Shaka. I was so nervous I had sweat dripping down my sides. They're going to pat you down and look in your mouth for contraband. You can't chew gum and you can't wear your watch." I was glad to be able to share what I could. I didn't have anyone to school me when I went on my first visit. "You'll be able to hug him and kiss him at the beginning of the visit, and again at the end. Are you going to kiss him?"

"I don't know," she said with a giggle.

We drove through the darkness, passing through Flint, then Saginaw, then Traverse City as the sun rose, singing along with our favorite artists. Prince. Jill Scott. Minnie Riperton. I was high on nothing but a few hours of sleep and adrenaline. We stopped for gas and bathroom breaks just before we reached the Mackinaw Bridge, the 5-mile-long bridge that connects the Lower Peninsula of Michigan to the Upper Peninsula. Four hours down, four more to go.

The hours slowed once we made it over the bridge. We drove through acres and acres of forest and farmland on long two-lane highways that stretched for miles. Our singing kept my mind off the monotony of the scenery.

Our energy was running low by the time we got to Baraga. No more sing-alongs and only a few words uttered between us for the last ten miles.

I couldn't wait to stretch my legs and take a hot shower. I'd booked us a room at the casino hotel, one of the few places to stay in the area. The prison and the casino are the lifeblood of this small white northern town. Most prisons are built in small towns just like this one. They bring government jobs with benefits and vending contracts and tourism to an otherwise struggling economy.

Just beyond the Welcome to Baraga sign, I saw the casino's

neon lights. When we pulled into the parking lot, it was nearly full. Cars with Michigan and Wisconsin license plates packed the lot and a charter bus sat at the back near the street. Trina and I checked into our room, showered, and dressed for our first visit.

The casino was less than a mile from the prison, but that short drive felt like forever. The summer sky was cloudy when we pulled onto the prison grounds. The parking lot was practically empty and the dark gray buildings looked even more ominous against the gray sky.

The butterflies in my stomach multiplied when I stepped out of the car. Visiting Shaka always brought me anxiety—each time there was a possibility my visit could be denied because of what I wore, or something happened on his end before I arrived. A fight. A riot. Anything was possible.

When Trina and I walked into the lobby, we were immediately greeted by the front desk officer. The room was sterile, the air stale. There was nothing but machines and chairs. After we signed in, the officer pointed us to a small corridor with two vending machines.

"You can get your snacks in there. There are no vending machines in the visiting room."

I looked at Trina, puzzled. I'd never heard of visitors buying their snacks beforehand. That meant I had to decide what Shaka was going to eat and drink for the next four hours, not knowing what he was in the mood for or how hungry he'd be. Inmates aren't allowed to use the vending machines; why take away one of the few choices they got to make? I wondered.

Once we got our snacks, the officer directed us to the control center so we could be processed through security. My excitement grew as the first set of security doors slid open. I walked through slowly and handed the officer my driver's license. I tried to seem unbothered. I remembered the day I walked into a prison for the first time, the day I met Shaka. Since then I'd gone through this process countless times, but I was still nervous as a female officer patted me down and checked the inside of my mouth. When she finished, she instructed me to stand by the second set of security doors, which led to the visiting room, and I stood there as Trina went through the same process.

The minute the visiting room door opened, I planted the biggest smile on my face and readied my body to leap into Shaka's arms. *I'm about to see my baby! I'm about to see my baby!* I repeated in my head, my heart beating faster. But when I turned the corner, Shaka wasn't there. My eyes searched the room for a full 30 seconds before I realized he hadn't been processed through security yet. I relaxed my smile, then locked my eyes on a table in the corner and sat down. Baraga's visiting room was much smaller than Cooper Street's—just three 4'-round tables with chairs. Inmates up north don't get many visits.

Trina and I exchanged nervous glances as we waited. Her friend hadn't been processed either. After five long minutes, the visiting room door opened, and my heart nearly leapt out of my chest. I stood up, straightened my clothes, and took a deep breath. When Shaka turned the corner, my face lit up. He smiled and instantly the tension in my body, the longing, left.

No matter how many calls we had or how long our letters, there was nothing like the connection we had on a visit. We laughed, held hands, played cards, and dreamed out loud. Dreaming was our escape—we could not change the past, we could not change the present, but the future was ours to shape. We imagined what we could create with our combined brilliance and passion. Books, movies, real estate, organizations that served the people. Once we were transported outside of the prison's walls and into the free world, *anything* was possible.

"The only limitation is our mind," I reminded Shaka.

"Indeed. We can think into existence anything we want, and believe me, baby, we're going to have everything we've dreamed of." Shaka was hungry for success and couldn't wait to come home to show the brothers inside what was possible if they put in the work. "I know the brothers are counting on me," he continued. His face turned serious. "I will not let them down or give them excuses to fail. Far too many buckle under the pressure. It takes an unshakeable belief in your vision to make it through the rough patches, and a lot of brothers don't have that, so when they meet with resistance, they quit believing. I refuse to be counted amongst those who quit. I will not be defeated or broken by the system."

We talked like this for four days. On the fourth day, when it was time to say our goodbyes, I hugged Shaka a little tighter. I kissed him, long and slow, as if it was our last. The next morning, Trina and I got back on the road.

Those four days were exactly what we needed, but they only left me craving more.

I knew the distance would be hard, but I didn't know that I would feel so hungry, like I needed to devour him. The feelings became a distraction.

"Right now, I feel like I'm just going through the motions, waiting until your next letter arrives in the mail or our next phone call. Baby, I am vulnerable right now, vulnerable to the realities of loving a man who's locked up. Before now, I was cool. I've been taking everything in stride, but now all of a sudden it seems I've been hit with a ton of bricks. Most days I don't even think about how much time you have left or how much longer we'll be apart physically, but sometimes, it just hits me. Reality sets in. Missing you has become as normal as waking up every morning and heading to work. I expect it. I plan for it. But some moments, I feel like I will explode if I miss you anymore.

"I don't know if I've been fooling myself all along or just in denial. I'd like to think it's been my strength that has kept me going, but in moments like these, I'm not so sure. I need and want to be with you RIGHT NOW! I can taste it. I can see it. You are always on my mind. Maybe if I stopped thinking about you, about us, as much as I do, I wouldn't miss you so much.

"I wish I could afford to come see you next week. I don't know if that would help or make missing you worse. Your energy is so calming. When we are together, just vibing, I feel so at peace. I love it when we just sit there in silence, holding each other. That's what I need right now. No words. Just you. Your presence. And only the sound of our hearts beating."

Winter was coming and since winters in northern Michigan can be brutal, I decided to make one more trip to Baraga before the snow came. This time, by myself. This time, on a budget. Funds were low, but spring seemed like a universe away.

I checked into a small, grungy hotel down the road from the prison. I'm sure the desk clerk knew why I was there. You won't find many Black people in Baraga. We are either going to the casino or the prison.

Once I showered and changed, I hopped back in the car. I wanted to be there when visiting hours started. We only had four hours.

"Remove your shoes," the officer barked at me. "Now take off your socks and lift up your feet."

He was rude. He had the power and he knew it. I knew he treated me that way because someone I loved was in prison, and that made me guilty by association. I also knew he treated me that way because I was Black and he had no respect for Black life. The only Black people he probably saw were on TV and in the prison he was hired to police.

I wasn't surprised by the officer's behavior, so I tried not to let him get to me. My smile was probably the only smile Shaka would see that day. I had to shake off whatever feelings I felt and put on my happy-to-see-you face. I knew Shaka had to do the same.

I walked through the Plexiglas door to the visiting room, and this time Shaka was already there waiting for me. It had been two months since we'd seen each other, and we sat like two lovestruck teenagers, holding hands and giggling the first 20 minutes of the visit.

We eased into conversation, snuggled together as close as we could without getting in trouble. I asked him about his day, he asked me about the drive up, and then we got caught up on all the things we couldn't squeeze into our weekly 15-minute calls or forgot to mention in one of our letters.

"I'm back writing," Shaka announced with excitement in his eyes. He hadn't been able to focus with the back-to-back transfers.

"That's good, baby. I'm happy to hear that."

"Yeah, I started working on the second volume of *Crack*. I'm really feeling the story right now, so I plan to write and write until I'm done, or I need to take a break from it. Once I'm done, it will free up space for me to finish the book about my life on the streets and in prison."

"I can't wait to read that one. I know you've been holding out on me because you want to save some things for the book."

He laughed. Shaka was a bit of a tease. He'd told me a great deal about his life but he'd kept some stories for his memoir.

Whenever we tired of the laughs and games, we'd talk about us. We'd grown so comfortable around each other that our conversations flowed from the lighthearted to the serious and back again.

"Sometimes your letters be a little extra," I admitted. "*My delicate little Nubian flower, as the sun gives birth to a new day, my love for you grows and expands in ways that continue to amaze me,*" I said, quoting him.

We laughed so loud the officer on duty looked up from whatever he was reading.

"You a hater."

"Baby, you know I love it. But we from the hood. Brothers don't talk like that."

"I'm just speaking from my heart."

Even though I knew Shaka was just trying to romance me, sometimes it felt like game. "I know, but every now and then doubt creeps in. Could be something I've seen on TV or read online." I looked down at the table and then back up at him. "I don't know what I'd do if you broke my heart. I would be devastated."

"Baby, I know. I would probably lose my mind were you to break my heart," he replied, his tone now serious. "I know I would never be able to love like this again. Words are too puny to express what you mean to me. You are the first person to get me on every level and that means the world to me."

I hung on the edge of his words. All his bravado, his street toughness was gone.

"Baby, I'd never break your heart," I said, looking directly into his eyes. "You are my soul mate, my forever. I don't know what I'd do without you."

We sat with the uncertainty for a moment. We couldn't have been more different, but our fears were the same. Rejection. Abandonment.

"Being in love is the hardest thing I have ever done," Shaka continued. "For years I thought that not feeling was a strength. I thought it made me a true warrior. I thought that indifference to emotions, to longings made me disciplined. When I started feeling those deeper feelings for you, a part of me got scared. It was that little boy inside that had been hurt before. But the man in me was like, 'Look, brother, this is who you want and need in your life,' so I conquered that fear. You may not realize how hard that was for me."

"I do. Believe me, I do. But isn't love beautiful?" I said, hoping to comfort him.

"It is. Never have I wanted to heap the full force of my love onto another soul." He grabbed my hand, then continued, "I love you completely, mind, body, and soul. But it feels like torture because I am limited in my ability to express the fullness of this love. On days when the torture is so intense I can feel it scraping the inside of my mouth, I cling to the hope of our slow forever. We are being tested, but I am confident that our love will remain unmoved."

There was some comfort in knowing we were both being tortured by the distance and the separation.

When visiting hours ended, I drove back to the hotel alone and crawled into bed to write.

no boundaries

> *love has no boundaries*
> *this, I know for sure*
> > *because it reached beyond the heavily guarded*
> > > *barb wired fences that keep you captive and*
> > > *blossomed like wildflowers through our letters*
> > *determined to grow, to live, to be*
> > *in spite of the rules and policies, mind games and*
> > > *politics that threaten its very existence*
> *it moves unnoticed through metal detectors and*
> > *surveillance cameras*
> *refusing to be locked down or denied freedom*
> *unaffected by the harshness of prison life*

daring to climb the mountain of hopelessness and despair
    that prison creates
it demands understanding
seeks compassion
it knows no boundaries

I called it an early night. There was nothing to do but dream anyway.

For three days it was just me and Shaka in the visiting room, lost in each other. On the afternoon of the third day, our last visit before I headed back home, we prepared ourselves for the long winter.

"Maybe we can do two calls a week," I proposed. "One on Sunday and one on Wednesday to break up the week."

"Are you sure?" He always asked if I was sure. He knew I had a tight budget and didn't want me to overextend myself.

"We'll see how it goes. If it gets to be too much, we can go back to our weekly calls on Sunday."

Traveling by myself left me with a lot of time to reflect. On the drive back to Detroit, I thought about our connection. Each time I thought we were closer than ever, it seemed our relationship grew new roots.

23

When I got home, I had no desire to cook, clean, eat, or even write letters. Nothing. I felt like a lazy bum. Whatever free time I had, I just seemed to waste it away laying on my couch pondering life. I didn't even have the energy to go to the gym, which was unusual for me. Working out was one of the good things that came out of my relationship with Rashad. It became one of the ways I loved on myself and was a distraction I looked forward to every day. There could be a fresh blanket of snow on the ground and I'd be at the gym first thing in the morning before I even shoveled my driveway. But those three days of visits changed everything. My appetite for Shaka's touch, his words, his energy was almost insatiable. Some days I just wanted to scream or cry or curse to the heavens, "Fuckkk!"

One afternoon, laying on my couch, avoiding the dishes, all the feelings I'd been feeling rushed in. I was mad at the system. I was mad at my bank account. I was mad at the weather. I was mad at myself. *This shit is hard. I don't know if I can do this for another two years. I can't. Why does my life have to be so hard? I just want to be happy.* The tears came slowly and I did not wipe them away. The release felt good.

And then guilt came.

I thought about those who had loved amid the brutality of slavery and Jim Crow, and I felt like a wimp. I hadn't endured half as much as they'd faced. I asked myself, can you imagine your love being stolen away and shipped across the Atlantic Ocean, or across state lines to a faraway plantation? Knowing you will never see them again. Knowing you will never hug them or make love to them again. Can you imagine your child being snatched from your breasts and sold like cattle? The pain in your gut that never goes away. Can you imagine listening, helplessly, as your love is raped by a savage slave master? Your heart breaking with each violent thrust. Knowing you cannot answer her cries for help. Can you imagine seeing your love hanging in a tree by a thick long rope wrapped around his neck, dangling lifelessly? The image forever stained in your mind, never getting justice, or relief from your memories?

I sat up. I wiped the tears, and somehow, from somewhere I mustered up a little more strength, a little more faith. I tried not to think about where Shaka was or how much time we had ahead of us and focused instead on the beauty of our love.

Shaka had shown me what love looked like. Because of him, I loved my body. Because of him, I loved the parts of me I'd been ashamed of. I loved me despite what the world said, or what the world did. I learned to love with my whole heart, to love hard as Toni Morrison reminds us in *Beloved*.

"In this here place, we flesh; flesh that weeps, laughs; flesh that dances on bare feet in grass. Love it, love it hard . . . More than eyes or feet, more than lungs that have yet to draw free air. More than your life-holding womb or your life-giving private parts, hear me now, love your heart. For this is the prize."

24

ven though I had prepared for my solo visit to be the last one until spring, we were having an unseasonably mild winter in Michigan. Week after week the high for the day was in the low- to mid-fifties. It seemed like a gift from Mother Nature, so I decided to make the trek up north again. The three-day Martin Luther King Jr. holiday weekend was approaching, and I would only have to take one day off from work.

"Are you sure? I know I told you I needed to see you, but I don't want you to feel pressured to drive up here."

"But I need to see you too. I can't wait four more months. The weather's been beautiful. We don't know how long it's going to be this mild."

We hadn't seen each other in three months. The memory of our last kiss returned. I thought of how he held me, how our tongues took their time. I thought of his smell, not sweet or sweaty, on my skin. I closed my eyes and imagined me there in the visiting room. The weekend couldn't come soon enough.

On Wednesday we had our midweek call, the bridge between our Sunday calls.

"The weather's not looking good," I told him. "The weatherman's predicting freezing rain. The temperatures are about to drop down in the thirties."

The phone grew silent.

"Really?" I could hear his excitement quieting. Shaka had been having a hard time. His son, Jay, who was now fifteen, was having problems in school and he'd always been close enough for his family to bring Jay up for a visit, so he could talk to him, father to son. But his family couldn't afford the long road trip and Jay's mother wasn't picking up the phone. All he could do was write Jay a letter, and now on top of that, I might not be able to visit.

There was also the monotony of prison. There weren't many programs or recreational activities at Baraga and visits didn't come often, so the guys were especially bored. Tensions were high and there were fights almost daily. Our visit would have provided a much-needed break.

I thought to myself, maybe I'm just tripping. The weather's not going to be that bad. I felt torn between Mama's warnings about safety and my need to see Shaka.

"What would you do?" I asked him. I didn't want to make the decision based solely on emotion—fear, or love.

"That's not a fair question. I want you to do what you think is right. I'm a guy and you know I'm a risk taker."

"I know. But sometimes I can be dramatic."

I decided to sleep on it. The weather might change, I said to myself.

Shaka called the night before I'd planned to leave.

"What's the word?"

"They're still saying it's going to rain and it's likely going to freeze. I don't want to chance it."

I knew Shaka would be disappointed. I was. But I had no idea it would affect him the way it did. He didn't want to finish the call.

I felt guilty. "My heart is heavy right now," I wrote him as soon as we got off the phone. "Knowing that I didn't come through for you when you needed me hurts like hell. Even though we knew my travel plans depended on what the weather did, just knowing that I let you down is the worst feeling in the world. I never want to hear the disappointment in your voice ever again."

I apologized profusely. There were few people Shaka could depend on. When I said I was coming for a visit, I did. When I said I'd send him money, I did.

Shaka said he understood, but my words weren't enough. He was mad at himself for getting excited, something he'd tried not to do in the sixteen years he'd been locked up. He wrote, "I was not disappointed in *you*. I would never want you to compromise your safety to come see me. I was disappointed because I couldn't *see* you. I was devastated because I had gotten so hyped up about seeing you that I'd forgotten things could change if the weather changed. I have had more disappointments than you can imagine so I try not to get too up about things. That way when things don't go the way I hope, I won't get too down. Sometimes excitement can blur our sight, and this just happens to be one of those times when I let my excitement get the best of me."

I wrote him back. "It's okay for you to feel what you felt. I would rather you allow yourself to feel those feelings than deny them or suppress them. You know that's not healthy. Your circumstances have forced you to deal with emotions differently and I respect that. I really do. I know there are some things I may never understand but just know I am here for you, to listen to your heart speak your truth, to help you process what you're feeling, to encourage and support you. I am here for you, baby."

I couldn't believe it when the weather turned out to be milder than forecasted. I beat up on myself for days because I had let my fear get the best of me. And then I remembered, everything happens for a reason. It wasn't meant for me to travel that weekend. I didn't question why.

That experience helped me understand Shaka better—how he handled disappointment, what visits meant to him, why he never got too excited about anything. And it made me appreciate the courage it took for him to love even more. "I know loving under these circumstances is hard on both of us, but I am now convinced that it is much harder on you," I wrote to him. "Our worlds are so vastly different. Your world is more cold, harsh, and unforgiving. There are few distractions to numb the pain and frustration of our oppression. Out here, we have the freedom of movement, which makes us think we are free. I don't have anyone watching my every move. I don't have to ask for permission. I can go to the movies or hang out with friends to dull the pain of missing you. You don't have that luxury."

I wanted to ease the sting of prison even more. I wanted to love Shaka even harder.

could always read the judgment on their faces.

"Are you crazy?"

"Have you lost your mind?"

"What's wrong with you?"

I know that's what people thought when I told them about Shaka, even though they didn't say it. Instead, they said nothing, their silence filling the room. And then the questions would start.

"What did he do?"

"How did you meet?"

"When does he get out?"

"Be careful" was usually how the conversation ended.

I had moments when I asked myself whether I was crazy. Am I crazy to wait? Am I crazy to expect happily-ever-after with a man who's been locked up half of his life? But our connection was almost cosmic, like two spirits meeting again. Sometimes love can't be explained.

I was never ashamed of our relationship, but I was selective about who I shared Shaka with. I didn't want anyone burying seeds of doubt in my mind or forcing their fears on me the way Mama did. That meant much of my excitement about the things Shaka said, or a beautiful moment we shared, I kept to myself. The last thing I needed was another opinion.

"You can't be in love. He's in prison. What can he do for you?"

"Girl, I ain't waiting on no man in prison. There are too many free men out here."

I didn't expect people to understand. He was in the most wretched placed on earth. And he'd taken a man's life. I just wanted them to trust my judgment. I wasn't reckless or irresponsible, or naïve.

"Your family loves you and they're just trying to protect you," Shaka reassured me.

"I know they love me, but it still hurts," I confessed. "They're judging you based on where you are, not *who* you are."

"I have prepared myself for the judgments I'll face when I come home."

"I know you have, you have to. But you know I'm protective of you."

"Don't worry about me. I don't give much weight to other people's opinions. I know what is in my heart. Just trust me, baby, I'm going to make this all worth it. They'll see."

"I know they will," I sighed.

I wanted them to see that not all men in prison are bad. I wanted them to see that our love was real, and I wasn't crazy for waiting.

26

Whenever Shaka called on a day other than Sunday or Wednesday, it usually meant he was being transferred. This time, he called on a Monday.

"They're riding me out tomorrow," he told me. He'd finally be leaving Baraga.

Shaka had been up north nine months. We hoped he'd be transferred downstate but knew there were no guarantees. He could be moved even farther north.

The next day, I didn't hear from him. He always called to let me know where he'd landed, so when that call never came, I knew something was wrong. Had he gotten into it with an officer? Or another inmate? Was he hurt? Then I worried that whatever had happened might impact his chances of parole.

Seven years earlier, Shaka had gotten into an altercation with an officer who refused to let him use the bathroom before count. They exchanged words and the officer pushed Shaka in the chest. Shaka punched him and ended up beating the officer unconscious. He was sentenced to two additional years for assault and sent to the hole indefinitely. He ended up spending four and a half years in solitary confinement.

That night, I cried myself to sleep.

The next day I was distracted at work thinking about Shaka. Every time my phone rang I'd answer, hoping it was him, or at least someone else calling to tell me he was okay, but nothing.

I decided to write to him. "It's hard not hearing from you and not being able to see you either. Damn them! With us unable to see each other regularly, I had begun to depend on our calls, so this is really hitting me hard. Having no way to communicate with you right now makes me appreciate your letters and calls even more. Baby, I'm telling you, when I see you again, I'm not going to know what to do with myself. I miss yo Black ass! I miss your touch, your kiss, the warmth of your body pressed against mine, your eyes and the way you look at me, your voice, your thoughts. I miss your everything. This is driving me crazy."

After a week of worry, a letter arrived from Shaka. He was at Marquette Branch Prison, one of the state's oldest prisons. He told me the guards had put him in the hole for no apparent reason as soon as he arrived. The counselor called him into his office later and told him that he was a security risk and therefore needed to be placed in the hole while the administration decided whether he would stay there or be transferred to another facility. Shaka suspected the administration was retaliating against him for a grievance he'd filed at Baraga against one of the officers who ordered him to do a job he wasn't assigned to.

For the next week, Shaka chronicled his ordeal in a series of letters. "When I got here, I told the officer that I hadn't eaten since 6am and he told me I would have to wait until dinner, which isn't until 4pm or so. The only thing I have eaten today is a banana." A few hours later he wrote, "4:20 pm. For dinner they gave me a grilled cheese sandwich, about 8 French fries, and 2 tablespoons worth of tomato soup. The dessert was pears mixed with lime Jell-O. The smell of state food served on plastic trays is nauseating. It's just something about that smell that I dislike. I only have about 10 sheets of paper, so I will have to write sparingly over the next couple of days. I really hope I am able to call or at least send out a letter to you before the week is out.

"My spirit is calm. I refuse to be broken. My main concern right now is you. It's times like this that make being in a relationship hard. Knowing how much this place hurts you is breaking my heart. All I want to do is protect and love you the way you deserve. I cling to the fact that this is temporary and if anyone can weather this storm, we can! I think of Mandela, George Jackson, and Assata and they keep me strong. Them, and your love. I feel your spirit here with me. You are warrior strong, yet you are tender, kind, and nurturing. Your softness makes me feel human."

With no communication for a week, I devoured his letter, rereading it multiple times. I was angry and sad, but relieved he was safe.

Shaka was on 23-hour lockdown for 10 days before they transferred him again. They sent him to Newberry Correctional Facility, which is about an hour north of the Mackinaw Bridge. This was an improvement over the eight-hour drive to Baraga, but in the process of transferring him they increased his security level, even though he hadn't done anything wrong.

"I am ready for war," I wrote him. "Just let me know what

you need me to do to support whatever grievance you're going to file. A phone call to Lansing, a letter, whatever."

We immediately got to work strategizing on how to get him moved back to a Level One facility. Level Two is like the Wild Wild West of prison. Many of the guys still have a lot of time left on their sentence, which means they're willing to take risks that guys in Level One, who are staring down freedom, wouldn't take. I wanted Shaka out of there before something happened to get him put in the hole, or worse.

"There were a couple of stabbings and they locked the yard down," Shaka wrote me days after he arrived at Newberry. "They had done a sweep of the prison a few days before that and recovered like 20 shanks, so it is real in the field right now. I need to get back down to Level One as soon as possible."

I got on the phone right away and spoke to anyone who would listen, from the warden's office to the department headquarters in Lansing. I kept notes on who I talked to and called weekly for updates. While I was calling Lansing, Shaka was in the law library researching the department's policies and operating procedures to back up the grievance he planned to file.

"I will not accept this laying down," Shaka wrote to me. "No matter what they do, I will not be thrown off the path of freedom. It feels good to know that I have a stand-up woman by my side. It's one thing to stand up for yourself and fight against injustice, but it is truly an honor to know that the woman I love is willing to go the distance with me. Adversity is the greatest revealer of character and with each conflict we face I am seeing more and more of who you are. You grow stronger and more committed and it is something I admire greatly."

We were growing into a strong couple, a force of resistance.

27

April in Michigan is still winter, but I couldn't wait any longer to see Shaka. Newberry is only five hours from Detroit, and even in winter weather, the trip felt doable.

This time, I made the trek with Maggie. Her husband was locked up and she'd gone on one of the bus visits I'd helped organize for families two years earlier. We became quick friends. When I told her about Shaka, she listened. She was the only person I knew who understood.

We planned a three-day trip. Gas prices in Michigan were among the highest in the country at the time, averaging around $3.50 a gallon, so we decided to drive my fuel-efficient Saturn instead of Maggie's old minivan. The day before, I went online to check the weather. Rain mixed with snow, it said. Temperatures were expected to be near freezing. *Damn*. I stared at the computer screen. I thought about the trip in January I'd canceled. All those emotions came rushing back. The sadness. The guilt. I'll just be careful, I thought to myself.

It was cold and gray when we left Detroit Good Friday morning. The rain waited for us in Traverse City and poured out of the sky. Once we got over the Mackinac Bridge the rain turned to snow, and then back to rain. I slowed down and tapped my foot on the brake. I could feel the ice beneath my tires. The oak and maple and spruce trees were just beginning to bloom and formed a canopy over the two-lane highway. The sun peeked through the branches but not enough to keep the snow that was now slush from freezing.

I inched through one small Michigan town after another, past farms and lonely gas stations, past small brick houses and big old wooden houses that had seen better days. I drove with my hands on the steering wheel at three o'clock and nine o'clock, my neck and shoulders and back knotted and tense from worry. I heard Shaka's voice, "You grow stronger and more committed."

"You good?" Maggie asked.

"Yeah, I'm good. I'm just going to take my time."

"That's right. We're in no hurry. We still have a couple hours before visiting hours start. He's going to be so happy to see you."

"Girl, I'm not gone know what to do with myself when I see him. It's been six months. But it feels like forever."

"I know. That's a long time. But now that's behind you." Maggie was encouraging. That was her way. She was a preschool teacher and had the biggest heart. She would take a carload full of women with her whenever she visited her husband and write letters to the parole board when the young men from her hood came up for parole.

There was nothing but trees and open land for miles and

then I saw a Pizza Hut, a McDonald's, and a gas station. The small-town trifecta. Just past the McDonald's was our hotel. I relaxed my arms and loosened my grip on the steering wheel.

"We're here," I sang. Maggie smiled. Her excitement was not like mine. She had been crisscrossing the state to visit her husband for years, so the novelty of visits was long gone.

Once we checked into our room, I took a shower and got dressed for our visit. I stared at myself in the mirror. My body was thin and frail and my face was red and covered in acne. It took everything in me to let Shaka see me like this, but my yearning to see him eclipsed any vanity I had left.

A year earlier, months before Shaka and I started corresponding, I'd had a severe breakout of acne. It was so bad that I didn't want to leave my house. I hid from the world. I went to work and came straight home. I was exhausted from all the stares. I would pretend I didn't see people staring at my face, not looking in my eyes when they talked to me, their gaze moving from one red swollen pustule to the next. Some people were visibly repulsed by my skin and even hesitant to hug me. I felt like a freak.

I couldn't figure out what had made my face break out so suddenly and so severely. I went to a dermatologist shortly after the breakout, and by the time Shaka and I had our first visit, my face had begun to clear up. But eventually I grew frustrated with the dermatologist. She was content with medicating the problem. She never once asked me about my diet, or whether I'd made any changes to my lifestyle. After a few months, I realized that my face would never heal completely if I continued to mask what was really causing such a horrible breakout. I imme-

diately stopped using the products the dermatologist had pre-
scribed and decided to figure out what was causing the acne.
On my own. I knew my body was trying to tell me something.

For weeks I researched the causes of acne. I tried vitamins.
I drank more water. I switched to black soap. I bought Queen
Afua's Rejuvenation Clay. And I got an earful from the sisters in
the community. "Have you tried this herbal remedy?" "I use this
or that for my skin, you should try it." Then one day I discovered a website that linked acne to an acid-alkaline imbalance
in the body. I had been vegetarian for more than ten years and
thought I had a pretty healthy diet, but I learned most of the
food I ate was acidic. I started eliminating one food at a time.
Bread. Dairy. Corn. Potatoes. Peanut butter. I'd wait a week or
two to see a difference, and then eliminate something else.

I had told Shaka what I was doing and warned him that I'd
lost some weight, but he was still surprised when he saw me.
My small frame was much smaller, the curves on me that he
liked disappearing.

"You've lost more weight than I thought," he said as soon as
we settled in.

"Really? You can tell?"

"Yeah, when I hugged you."

We talked about the weight loss. We talked about the
shame.

"You are the most beautiful woman in the world to me. I see
your true beauty."

"Thank you, but I don't feel beautiful," I replied, tears well-
ing up in my eyes.

"That's understandable. But what I see could never be

28

Every chance Shaka got, he sent me articles from *Black Enterprise* or excerpts from the wealth-building books he'd read. Books like *Think and Grow Rich* and *Rich Dad Poor Dad*. He helped me see what was possible and inspired the budding entrepreneur in me.

"Success is based on a combination of factors," he once explained. "The first factor is having a vision, the second is having a well-focused plan, and the third is having the courage and determination to see your plan through. There are some intangibles like timing and opportunity but the only thing that stands between us and success is us."

Publishing Shaka's work was our first business venture together. I was blown away by his storytelling skills when I read *Crack*, the first manuscript he sent me. I knew I had to help him live his dream.

"Which one should we publish first?" he asked after I read his second novel.

"I really loved *Crack*. That one was fire. I think in terms of building the brand, that's the book we should start with." Shaka had written *Crack*, the story of a Detroit detective who tries to solve the murder of his childhood friend, by hand when he was in solitary confinement. Once he was released from the hole, he typed the entire manuscript on a word processor, printing the pages when the memory filled up, and then typing some more.

Shaka's books were raw and gritty but he didn't glamorize the streets. He wanted his work to show the cultural impact of that life. "The novels are like keys that will open the doors of opportunity for me to do what I was called to do," Shaka explained. "*Crack* is a good story, but it isn't the most important book I've written. It is important in terms of creating a brand. Once they are hooked on the brand, we will be able to infuse them with revolutionary ideas that will dramatically change the way they see themselves and our community. This is so much bigger than us putting a few books out."

We held our business meetings on paper, but we had to be careful not to raise any suspicions in the mailroom because inmates aren't allowed to own or operate a business. Shaka didn't have access to the Internet and didn't fully understand what it was—he'd gone to prison in 1991, before the world wide web was a thing—but he knew it was a great business resource.

"Check out these websites for me," he'd ask, followed by a page-long list.

I'd do the research and either provide a summary in a letter or print the pages, no more than ten at a time, for him to read himself. He was like a sponge. Whatever I sent him inspired more questions, more ideas. And more research. He wanted to learn everything he could about the book business so he could hit the ground running when he came home.

"Amazon has a print on demand company. See what they're talking about."

"Okay, I'll look into it and get back to you."

"And see what you can find about the pros and cons of print on demand and traditional publishing. I think we should weigh all of our options."

I leaned on my experience working with Malik's bookstore in Detroit and Shaka drew on his experience in the streets selling dope. It was the perfect marriage of our skills.

I knew how hard it would be for Shaka to get a job once he was released, so I poured my energy into making his dream happen. Mine could wait. He'd be rebuilding his life after nearly twenty years in prison. I wanted him to have something to come home to.

Once we started working on the business, it was as if he'd been given new life. It gave him hope. "One of the first things you said when we started building was that you would help me. That meant everything. It wasn't so much that you were willing to help, but that you saw my worth as a human being. Never once have you made me feel like a charity case, or feel like I was the crime I committed. It means the world to me to have you by my side. Baby, I am telling you, once we get the first book done we are going to be off and running. There will be no limits to what all we can do with this company."

But hope wasn't enough. We needed capital. I estimated that we'd need about $4,000 for our first print run.

I asked Shaka, "Do you think your family would be willing to support this project with a financial contribution? Maybe a hundred dollars per person? Is that too much?"

"That's a great idea, baby. I'll see what I can do."

"Whatever is needed beyond what you can collect, I'll make up the difference," I continued. "I may be able to borrow some money. Whatever the case, I'll hustle up on it. I just can't do it all by myself."

Shaka was able to raise $900. We needed another $3,000 to go to print. We considered just about every fundraising scheme possible, from selling gift baskets to calendars, to selling a percentage of the company. But these ideas would take months to turn enough profit.

"I can use my credit card," I proposed. I didn't want money to get in the way of making his dream happen.

"Baby, I don't like the idea of you carrying the financial burden," Shaka replied. "You don't have to do this. We'll figure it out."

"I'm not saying charge everything to my credit card, just the printing costs. I can use the cash you raised toward the other costs, like the postcards and bookmarks and maybe even the website."

Finally, he agreed.

We went to work immediately. He had a guy draw the concept he had for the book cover and sent it to me. A crack pipe, a broken detective's badge, and the Detroit skyline. I shared the drawing with a graphic designer I knew.

"You think you can work with this?"

"Yeah, no problem."

"Cool. I don't want the drawing to box you in. It's just a concept. Feel free to use your creativity."

It felt like Christmas morning when I checked my email a week later and saw the subject line: DRAFT COVER CRACK VOLUME 1. The moment I saw the designer's rendering of Shaka's concept, I got choked up. I thought about everything Shaka had been through and how much this project meant to him. I started a letter. "I am so excited right now. I can't wait to talk to you Sunday night. I got the first draft of the book cover today and it's hot! I almost cried. Seeing the drawing come to life just made everything real. I can't wait for you to see it. I know you're going to love it. I see a few things I want to change, but overall I am very pleased with the product. I suggest that when you call me Wednesday night, bring the draft with you to the phone so we can critique it together with it right in front of us. I would rather discuss this kind of thing by phone so that we have a faster turnaround. That way I can get back to the brother on Thursday with our feedback and he can make the changes within a few days."

I printed an 8.5" × 11" version of the cover and rushed to the post office. We'd been careful about how much we discussed on the phone, but I didn't think there would be a problem with him getting the book cover.

"Gorgeous, I love it," Shaka said as soon as I answered the phone. "You should have seen me when I pulled the cover out of the envelope. My heart was beating fast, and as soon as I looked at it, I hopped off my bunk with a big-ass smile on my face like, damn. I stood there for about five minutes just staring at the cover and all the while I was thinking about you and how amazing you are. When I finally broke out of my trance, I showed it to this brother in my cube and he started smiling. Then I shared it with a few more brothers and they all got hyped, which of course made me more and more excited. You the best, baby." There was an electricity in his voice I hadn't heard before. "I will probably cry like a baby when I hold the actual book in my hand for the first time."

It felt good to see him excited.

We turned our attention to the inside of the book. I had to retype, edit, and format the manuscript he'd typed on his word processor. Editing was time consuming. The unedited version of *Crack* was more than 300 pages. We went through a few rounds of revisions, me sending him the fully edited manuscript and him sending me his feedback in a series of letters. Once I made the final edits, the book was ready to send to the printer. We agreed to start with 1,000 copies.

We weren't just dreaming anymore. We were making it happen.

29

A couple weeks later, Shaka was transferred from Newberry to Ojibway Correctional Facility, a Level One prison in the northwestern tip of the Upper Peninsula. All those calls had worked.

We had planned to see each other that weekend but Ojibway was nearly ten hours away on the border of Wisconsin. Suddenly Baraga didn't seem so bad. I didn't want to do that ten-hour drive alone, so once again we had to wait until I found somebody to ride with me.

Days after Shaka arrived, he called me excited. "My guy D is here and he said his girl would ride up with you. We've known each other since middle school and we were at a couple joints together early in my bit." I didn't want to ride with someone I didn't know, but I trusted Shaka's judgment. "My main concern is your safety and well-being. There are guys who would have their woman bring drugs in and won't say anything to the person they're driving up with. Then if they get caught, the police will be looking at us suspiciously and I would never put you in that kind of situation. D's good people."

"Cool, give his girl my number."

Our one-year anniversary was coming up and I wanted to plan a trip for that weekend. The girlfriend called me and we started making plans. We decided to head out around midnight on a Thursday evening and drive through the night so we could make the visiting hours on Friday, which started around two o'clock. The night we were supposed to leave, the girlfriend called, frantic.

"I'm waiting on my cousin to get off work. She supposed to keep my kids and she hasn't called yet."

"Okay, keep me posted. I'm ready when you're ready."

Two hours later, she called again.

"I'm sleepy . . . blah, blah, blah . . . I don't like to drive at night."

Wait, what? I was pissed. I tried not to show it. "I don't want you driving if you're sleepy. I can drive first."

"We could stop and get a room if we get too sleepy," she suggested.

I thought about it. Two women driving in the middle of the night, stopping in the middle of nowhere at some remote hotel in northern Michigan. "Nah. You want to take a nap and leave around 4am?"

"Yeah, that sounds good."

I called four hours later and she didn't answer. I called again and again, and she never picked up. I was livid.

Shaka called me on my cell phone around 7am with excitement in his voice. He thought we were on the road.

"I'm at home," I said when he asked how much longer we had.

"What? What happened?"

I told him everything. "I'm real fucked up right now. I wanted to see you so bad this weekend. This is exactly why I didn't want to travel with somebody I don't know."

"Damn, I can't believe she played you like that. I'm sorry, baby. I'mma holla at D when the yard opens."

"You don't need to apologize. But D needs to talk to his girl. For real."

Hours later, the girlfriend called. No apology. No explanation. She was ready to get on the road.

"Nah, I'm good. At this point, we wouldn't make visiting hours today. And that means we'd only get to visit Saturday. I don't want to drive ten hours just to see him for a few hours." Sunday was our anniversary and I wanted to spend that day together, but she'd told me she had to be back on Sunday.

"I knew some shit like this was gone happen," she said, like it was my fault.

"What are you talking about? You were the one saying you were sleepy. You were the one who didn't answer the phone this morning."

"I was ready to go last night."

I stopped listening. She was what Mama called a bullshit artist. I was even more pissed.

That weekend, I tried not to think about what happened. On our anniversary, we splurged on calls—five to be exact, two in the morning and three that night. A few days later, I got a letter from Shaka that he had probably mailed the day I was supposed to head up to Ojibway. He was hyped about our visit. "Baby, I am so excited to see you, touch you, hold you, and to hear you laugh. You are truly my ride or die queen and I appreciate all that you are," he wrote. I winced as I read the rest of his letter. I got mad all over again, but mostly there was guilt. He had allowed himself to get his hopes up. *I should have gone.* I thought about how much that weekend meant to us. I thought about how heartbroken he was when I told him I wasn't coming. I'd vowed I'd never disappoint him again.

I wrote Shaka. "Your letter was so hard to read. I felt guilty. I felt selfish. But baby, I don't regret my decision. I chose to listen to that little voice in me that said, 'This girl is drama. Beware.' Believe me, that wasn't an easy decision to make but I had to trust my gut, and each time I make a decision that honors that little voice, I celebrate that. I know it meant we didn't get to celebrate our anniversary together, but I keep reminding myself everything happens for a reason."

I didn't know what that reason was, but in just one year, Shaka had been transferred seven times and moved 600 miles away from me. We had grown stronger and more committed and more in love, and I trusted that all of this was part of God's plan for us.

30

There was usually nothing but junk mail in the post office box I'd opened for the business, but one day there was an envelope from the Michigan Attorney General's office marked CERTIFIED MAIL. My heart dropped into my stomach. I opened the letter as soon as I got into my car. The state had filed a lawsuit against Shaka. They wanted ninety percent of the royalties from *Crack*. I was being subpoenaed.

My mind started racing. *I got to talk to Shaka*. I couldn't call him, and a letter would take days for him to get, so I waited anxiously for him to call me.

"I got a letter the other day," I told Shaka when he called a couple days later. I chose my words carefully. I knew our call was being recorded.

"That's some bullshit. I have worked their slave wage jobs for sixteen years and now they want to demand ninety percent of what we've put one hundred percent into. I bet the mailroom clerk at Newberry saw the book cover and told the warden."

We couldn't talk much about the lawsuit on the phone, so we took to pen and paper to discuss strategy and decide how we'd respond. Shaka's years as a prison law clerk came in handy. He knew what language I needed to use. I responded to the subpoena with what Shaka and I thought would appease them. "Mr. White has decided to donate the proceeds from the sale of his book to a charity of his choosing."

And then we waited.

I was nervous. I'd never been sued or subpoenaed. Would I have to testify in front of a judge? What if I say the wrong thing? How would this affect his chances of parole?

"I don't want you to be afraid of the State," Shaka told me. "We have done nothing wrong. We have dared to dream. I want you to move in the spirit of courage. Don't let your desire to see me paroled cause you to operate out of fear. I would rather die in here as a man than to submit to something I know is wrong. I will not beg or plead with them to let me go. We know what the mission of my writing is, and I will not back down."

When the case was heard, the judge ruled in the State's favor. Michigan law allows the Department of Corrections to seize ninety percent of an inmate's income to cover the cost of his or her incarceration. They calculated the cost of housing and feeding Shaka for every year he had been locked up. The total was close to one million dollars.

The lawsuit dampened our spirits. We had big plans for *Crack*, but we chose not to promote the book inside Michigan prisons. We'd wait for Shaka to come home. That wasn't an easy decision. Shaka had a name and reputation in prison that would make sales easy. We knew the book would do well and word-of-mouth would help us promote the book in the streets. But we didn't want any more problems.

Shaka was frustrated. One night on the phone, he started venting. "The only thing I have ever wanted to do is give my children and the brothers in here an example to live by. I wanted to show them that no matter what you are faced with in life, you can overcome it if you believe in yourself."

I interrupted him, "You'll still be able to do that. We'll do what we can with the fed system."

He got quiet. I could hear the wheels turning in his head. "I refuse to come home broke, Eb."

"Listen, when you come home, whatever money you make on book sales you can keep. I'm able to take care of all the bills with my income. The costs for visits and the phone won't be an issue anymore so we'll be good."

"I'm not trying to be a burden to anyone when I come home."

"You wouldn't be a burden. This is what couples do." This is what my mama had to do.

"I know you don't want me to feel pressure to contribute to the household right away. But you have to understand, my personality won't allow me to be any other way. I am not the dependent kind of guy. I'm a go-getter and I am not going to settle for mediocre. I know it's going to take some time for me to get on my feet, but I'm going to do everything in my power to make this work."

couldn't afford to drive to Ojibway by myself so I started looking online for other ways to visit Shaka up north. Plane, train,
bus, something. I felt trapped. The weather was beautiful, but
I couldn't just jump on the road when the mood struck.

One night I discovered an online discussion forum for individuals and families connected in some way to the prison
system. Moms. Wives. Former inmates. There were forums for
those seeking legal help, or treatment resources. Forums for
those with a loved one on death row, or life in prison. I landed
in the Michigan forum, in a chat room where families could ar-
range carpools or ask questions about specific prisons. I wasn't
interested in riding with someone neither of us knew but the
other threads intrigued me, made me somehow feel I wasn't
alone. The threads started:

What is it like inside Ojibway?

First visit to Ojibway, any advice?

Having trouble getting married at Ojibway. Need help.

I clicked on every thread and then found my way into the

forum for wives and girlfriends. It felt like a life vest had been thrown to me. I stayed up past midnight that first night, reading thread after thread, and then again the next night. There were hundreds of discussions about everything you could imagine, from "Is he using you?" to "How do you pass the time?"

I found a sisterhood in the MWI, or Met While Incarcerated, group and that's where I spent most of my time. All the women in this group had met their boyfriend or husband after he'd gotten locked up. It was comforting to read about their struggles and how they coped with the loneliness, the judgments, the alienation. I didn't feel by myself on an island. I felt connected. I felt understood.

But there were some in the wives and girlfriends forum who thought women like me, who didn't know their man before he got locked up, were delusional. They said relationships like Shaka and I had weren't real. These women knew their husband or boyfriend before he went in, and in many cases, had been together for years. Some of them had children together. They *knew* their man, they insisted.

"If you met someone while incarcerated, there's just no way you can know him as well as if you'd met him outside prison walls. I got to see how my husband interacted with other people, how he handled stress. Prison is stressful but when you get to the 'real world,' that's where the stress really comes into play . . . bills, children, sex, employment, compromising."

They held nothing back.

"How can you miss something you never had? Yes, you yearn to have your man near, yes you love him, and you connect on an emotional level, but we have all of that plus the physical."

Some of them sounded like my mama.

"I believe a man you met before incarceration can lie about anything, but it's a lot harder to pull wool over my eyes when we're together all the time, we're living in the same house, our finances are tied together, and I see how you interact with people in different situations. When you meet someone while incarcerated, you're taking a chance on the person getting out and having a whole different personality. It's not that they even have this new personality, it's just that they were putting on a front the whole time because it's easy to do when you only have to talk to someone during visits, in letters, and on the phone."

Initially I was just a fly on the wall watching the women go back and forth, mumbling my disagreement. Then finally after a couple weeks, I started commenting. "Whether you are MWI or MBI, communication can make or break a relationship. In my opinion, a couple who has an open, honest line of communication is more secure than any other relationship. That couple will be more likely to meet challenges head on and work through them together as a team. They are more likely to express their thoughts and feelings with each other, good, bad, or ugly. Having children does not guarantee shit. Living together doesn't either. You can marry him, have a rock on your finger, have his baby, and wait twenty years, but if you don't communicate well, none of that means jack."

I knew Shaka and I were good. We communicated well and resolved arguments quickly. I was confident in our love.

I shared more and more of my relationship with Shaka as I grew comfortable. I didn't have anyone to talk to in the beginning, when the doubts crept in, so I welcomed the opportunity to share my thoughts with the women who were new to their relationship. "Love is a beautiful thing, ain't it? Love seeks understanding, forgiveness; it inspires greatness. Loving a man in prison is not easy given all the misperceptions and fears society has about prisons, but when that man is considered a 'violent offender' it's even harder to look past the judgments of others and into the heart of the man. You can't let what's right and good for other people determine what feels right and good for you. There are only two emotions in life . . . love and fear. Everything else is rooted in one of these two emotions. It's up to us to decide which one we will allow to shape our life. I pray you choose love."

I got online every night. It felt good to have a community of women to help me ride out the time. I was captivated by some of their stories. There was the woman who met her man when he misdialed her number calling collect from the county jail, and the woman from the UK who met her man on a pen pal site for U.S. inmates. I saw parts of me and Shaka in their relationships. But I didn't have the fears that many of them had. "I think it's sad that we've come to expect men to cheat," I wrote in one of the countless threads on cheating. "And when they do, we make all kinds of excuses for them. 'He was in prison' or 'That's just the way men are.' I think that's a bunch of BS. As women, we have to raise the bar on how we will be treated and what we will allow in our relationships. We typically go for the guys who are emotionally immature and simply lack basic integrity. A MAN has integrity and wouldn't think of cheating on his woman. And that's the kind of man I got by my side. No doubt."

The stories I read online made me feel more connected to Shaka, but it was the stories on *Lockup*, the MSNBC documentary series, that transported me inside Shaka's world. Their cameras showed me things I'd only been able to imagine. I saw the inside of a cell for the first time. The thin, hard mattress, a window no bigger than an envelope, the concrete slab desk. I heard the heavy steel doors open and close, controlling the movement of bodies. I listened to the inmates and the officers describe the violence and thought about some of the stories Shaka had shared. For that hour, I was there with him. Not just in the visiting room, but in the spaces beyond the Plexiglas.

"Tell me what it's like," I wrote Shaka, curious about the things the *Lockup* cameras couldn't show me. "What do you do when you first wake up? How far is the bathroom from your cube? What times are your meals served? Do you usually eat meals by yourself? How early can you leave your unit to go work out?"

Shaka wrote me a detailed letter in reply, chronicling his day. "When I first wake up, I usually lie in the bed for half an hour, meditating and thinking about life. Once I have cleared my mind, I get up and straighten my bunk area. I am on the back side of the unit on 'A' wing and my cube is the last one, so I have to go down the hall to use the bathroom. Shift changes at 7am and they do count at about 7:05am. Once count clears ten minutes or so later, we are allowed to go to the bathroom. They usually call early chow ten minutes later for the guys going out on public works, gate pass, and school. Ten minutes after that they call our wing, so usually breakfast is served around 7:30am. Our wing is first for breakfast and lunch and last for dinner. When we eat in the chow hall, we are all basically crammed on top of each other, so we have to eat together.

Today's breakfast was cereal and peanut butter and jelly with toast, milk, and juice. That is one of the better breakfasts they serve. I will have to get you a menu. We have four basic rotations and it is usually the same at every joint with minor variations, so I have been eating the same food over and over for sixteen years. I appreciate you asking these questions. I don't like complaining or sounding like I am complaining. This is the price I had to pay for the life I lived."

I tried to picture the places Shaka mentioned and compared them in my mind to the images on *Lockup*: the inside of his unit, the chow hall, the yard. Whenever he crossed my mind during the day, I'd think about where he might be and what he might be doing and I felt closer to him even though he was far away.

3 2

ventually our letters started to slow down, mostly my letters to him. One day I got a letter from Shaka, frustrated again that he hadn't gotten a letter from me. "A note with 'Love, Eb' would have been enough to make this dreary day bright and lively. A small card with a smiley face on it saying 'Hi' would have really made a world of difference. See, there are days when I want to hear from you, which is most days, but then there are days like today when I needed to hear from you and no one else. They could have brought me a stack of mail the size of the Yellow Pages and it would not have mattered unless there was an envelope in the pile with your name on it. But this isn't really about mail, it's about a deeper need that only you can meet. It just so happens that on this day the only way that it could have been met was through the mail."

Shaka had been up north for more than a year and I was tired. I feared a part of me was beginning to shut down or become numb so that I wouldn't feel the pain of missing him.

numb

is this what they meant when they said love hurts?
how could they have known my heart would ache so
        much?
that my tears would become a welcomed release
      releasing the frustration, and loneliness
my heart yearns to be near you
yet knows there are no promises
my body yearns to be held, to touch and caress you
but I am numb
my senses deadened from the sting of my reality
our intimacy limited to fantasy-filled letters, erotic phone
      calls and timed embraces
but this, however precious it is, is never enough
how could it be with a love so supreme?

There were times when Shaka's letters didn't move me. "Not a moment passes without a thought of you dancing through my mind," he wrote one day. "Your love is a sacred gift from the gods, or maybe from some long-forgotten ancestor who knew only a woman like you could love and understand me." Words that usually made me smile did nothing for me—they were simply letters on a page. I wrote him. "Your words will never be substitutes for your touch, no matter how colorful or poetic."

I wasn't in the mood to do the things we'd always done to keep the spark in our relationship. I did not want to flirt. I did not want to have phone sex. I did not want to write a steamy love letter.

Shaka took it personal. He thought I didn't want *him* anymore.

"What's wrong? You not feeling me?"

It wasn't him; it was *everything*. The distance, the Michigan Department of Corrections, the phone bill, and the doubts in my head.

"I'm simply not in the mood to have sexual conversations," I told him. I wasn't even in the mood to masturbate. I couldn't put into words all that I was going through right then, but I told him, "I'm going through a thing. I miss you, I want you, and I yearn for your touch and your presence every day. I am overwhelmed at work and my man isn't here to comfort me and make love to me at the end of the day. Forgive me if I'm not myself right now. I want long kisses, not long letters."

I had made a conscious choice to be celibate, but it was harder than I expected. I wanted to be touched in all the parts he couldn't reach, the parts his letters couldn't satisfy. I wanted more. I missed sex. I imagined, almost daily, what our first time would be like. I daydreamed about how he'd feel inside me, how easily we'd find our rhythm, how long we'd make love, how we'd hold each other as we drifted to sleep.

Shaka said he understood what I was going through. He had been sexually frustrated early in his bid. "It is by far one of the hardest adjustments I had to make. I had to condition myself mentally to go without the pleasure of sex. What can I do to help you in this area? Your complete happiness means the world to me. Do you need me to write more or less? Do you need me to be more understanding? Whatever I can do to help just let me know. I'm here for you."

"This too shall pass," I told him. "No matter how horny I get, I can wait." I knew another man wasn't the answer. Shaka was the only man I wanted.

"I promise you I will make love to you in a way that will make you forget about the hard part of our journey. I will love away all of the years of frustration and loneliness. I will love you the way a woman is supposed to be loved."

Together, we found ways to deal with not being able to have sex. We focused on our spiritual and emotional growth as a couple, and this brought us closer. We fasted together. We read books together. We continued to build the foundation for our future.

Though the distance was difficult, I was getting the space I needed to heal. Being celibate made me realize that I often had sex because it was expected, not always because I wanted to. I had never experienced nonsexual intimacy with any of the guys I'd dated. The idea that kissing and cuddling didn't have to lead to sex, that I could be intimate without it going *there*, was foreign to me. With Shaka, there were no expectations. We couldn't do more than cuddle and hold hands. I learned to just be.

In those moments between longing and resignation, I realized that sex wasn't what mattered. It was what we created in its place that mattered most.

33

The New Year carried the promise of our first year on the outside together. Shaka would finally be seeing the parole board. We spent New Year's Eve on the phone sharing our goals. We were giddy.

"This time next year, you'll be at home here with me!"

"Fa sho. Our time is here, baby. Everything we've dreamed of is about to be ours."

"I know! And I can't wait. September can't come soon enough."

"For years I've held my feelings in check when it comes to getting out. When I felt myself getting excited, I would reel it in. It wasn't that I didn't want to enjoy those feelings. I just wanted to maintain some balance and not drive myself crazy. But now I sit here and all I can do is think about getting out. I'm ready."

"You know it's all I think about," I laughed. "But seriously, we got to get our minds right. There's a lot that needs to be done so we have to be focused."

"Right, we need to pull everything together for my parole hearing, get the book out there, and make final preparations for my homecoming."

Joy suddenly rushed through me. "Babyyyy!" I screamed in the absence of words more profound or beautiful.

"What?"

"This shit is almost over. I can't wait to start counting down the weeks and days."

We had to say our goodbyes around eleven o'clock. The operator interrupted us. "You have one minute."

"Happy New Year, baby!"

"Happy New Year, gorgeous."

I lit a candle and opened my journal. I looked back on the year and thought about what I'd learned. I started writing. "1) Listen to my spirit, that little voice inside that guides and instructs, aka my first mind, when I need to make an important decision or need clarity on an issue. 2) I am worthy to be loved completely. Unconditionally. No, I'm not perfect but I am a unique and wonderful expression of God and I am deserving of all the love and life the Universe has to offer. 3) Patience is a strength. I've always known I was strong, but I never knew just how strong. I have learned to lean on my faith and draw from a well of strength that runs deep." Once I finished, I closed my eyes and prayed, and ten minutes later, pen still in hand, I fell asleep.

The next week I called Lansing. We had been waiting for Shaka to be placed in a ten-month-long program that he needed to complete before he could be paroled. The Assaultive Offenders Program (AOP) provided group psychotherapy and was required for anyone serving time for any of a number of violent crimes including armed robbery, assault, and murder. Thousands of inmates were required to complete this program but there were only a handful of psychologists across the state trained to facilitate the weekly sessions. This created a massive backlog and meant that some guys didn't finish the program before they saw the parole board. I'd spent months making calls trying to get Shaka into AOP but kept getting the runaround.

"Oh, he'll definitely be in the class before his ERD."

"But his ERD is September twenty-six. It's January. The class is ten months long. If he doesn't get in a class now, he won't be done before he sees the board."

"There are no groups starting this month. We'll have a group starting in mid-March at Ojibway. There's a good chance he'll be in that group."

"Can he be transferred to another facility, so he can get in a group that starts earlier?"

"Ma'am, there's a list and there are still a lot of people ahead of him."

I wished there was something I could do. "This is so fucking frustrating," I wrote Shaka. "I feel so helpless at the hands of the State. Nothing I do is helping. This shit is like a Rubik's cube. I know you're used to this bullshit, but I'm having a hard time dealing with this. The system is broken."

Eventually, frustrated, I let go. "I have decided to just surrender to the Creator's will and go with the flow. There is little else I can do at this point." *Everything is in divine order*, I kept telling myself.

I tried to reassure Shaka, and myself. "I believe this is all going to work out. Everything happens for a reason. I know it's hard to sit back and watch other guys get transferred, but I believe there are a number of things the Creator is trying to line up for us so that wherever you get transferred, it's going to be a good spot in terms of the officers, the administration, the other captives. And we want whoever leads your class to be a cool person who will give you an excellent report. We want these last ten months to be as stress free as possible. We are blessed, baby, and I continue to have faith that the Creator and the ancestors are looking out for our best interests and you'll be somewhere that'll make it worth this long wait."

"I knew this part of the journey was going to be tough, but I just never thought I'd be this close to my ERD still waiting to get into AOP. This not knowing is killing me but I know the Creator's got our back."

While we waited, I sent Shaka a list of possible interview questions that I'd found online to help him prepare for his parole hearing. What would you do if you were granted parole? What changes have you made since being in prison that can assure you will not re-offend? I also found some sample parole letters and drafted a letter to the parole board in support of Shaka's release. I spoke about how we'd met, how he'd transformed his life, and his plans once he was released. I ended the letter, "I am impressed with the man Mr. White has become and am honored to write you on his behalf. He has a beautiful spirit with a deep love for his family and community and will be a great asset upon his release. I am hopeful that you will see the positive changes in him that so many others have seen and grant him the parole that he has earned. Mr. White is more than ready to serve his community and looks forward to being a positive, productive member of society. Please give him that opportunity."

I sent the letter to Shaka and he was beaming when he called me.

"You the shit. This is perfect, baby."

"Thank you. This is just a draft. I'm going to make a few more changes."

"Cool. So who else should we get to write a letter?"

Letters of support from family and friends and community members help the parole board paint a picture and show the board that the inmate won't be alone on an island when they are released. We wanted to show that Shaka had a strong support system that included his family and the community. I answered, "I'll ask Malik and Mama Aneb if they'll write a letter. And maybe I can get a letter from Councilwoman Joann Watson and Commissioner Bernard Parker. Bernard's the chair of the Wayne County Community Corrections Advisory Board, so something from him would be a good look."

"Okay, I'll talk to my father and my aunt Bebe and I'll see if one of my siblings will write a letter. I'm sure Tom Lagana from Chicken Soup for the Prisoners' Soul will write one too."

Shaka sent me whatever certificates he had accumulated from the classes he'd taken inside and I created a packet for the parole board that included the certificates, some of his published essays, his transcript from Montcalm Community College where he'd earned credits toward an Associate's Degree, and the letters of support we'd gotten. Then I started calling Lansing again. I'd said I was going to let go, but I couldn't. Shaka was less than six months away from seeing the board and he still wasn't in AOP. One day, I called the warden's office to see if I could get some answers.

"Honey, his chances of getting parole the first time is probably one percent," the woman who answered the phone told me.

My heart sank. I knew every case was different, I knew Shaka was different, but her words stung. I felt like giving up.

When I told Shaka what she'd said, his words put me at ease. "Baby, I can feel your frustration when it comes to dealing with these people. However, I don't want you to ever allow them to get you discouraged. We are warriors. As long as you are mindful of the nature of our enemy, nothing they do should surprise you. Though it may not seem like your efforts are bearing fruit, they do serve a purpose. Words and thoughts are like seeds. The more seeds you plant, the better the chances that something will sprout. When I hear them say things like I only have a one percent chance, I smile inside. The reason I smile is because I know that my being here is a result of that one out of a billion sperm making it through. And I know I represent one percent of the captive population. Trust me, baby, there aren't many captives going to the board as prepared as we are. There also aren't that many brothers who have put in the kind of work I have to become a true asset to our community. So sometimes being one percent isn't all that bad. I mean, think about it. We have a supreme love based on a connection that is rare. The odds of us connecting the way we did under the circumstances is probably less than one percent. Trust me, we haven't gone through what we've gone through for nothing. We were brought into each other's life for a reason. There is a plan in place for us that is greater than our current circumstances.

"I know I'm coming home. I can't imagine the parole board not granting me a parole when they look at all of the information in front of them."

I wrote Shaka back, encouraged. "I know we have the Creator and the ancestors on our side. We will defy the odds. I feel it in my heart and soul." I was optimistic. Anything less would mean defeat, he told me.

But a few weeks later, when Shaka mentioned that his boy D was two years from maxing out, all the optimism I had flew out the window. Reality started to settle in. D had a 10- to 20-year sentence and had been denied parole, or flopped, eight times. Shaka had a 40-year tail on his sentence. What if they flopped him every year like they did D and he never got paroled? Could I wait twenty more years if it came to that? I thought I'd be waiting two years and that seemed like forever.

I had never considered the possibility that Shaka could get flopped. He had given me nothing but optimism.

"We never talked about the what ifs," I wrote Shaka. "I wish we had. That's not to say I would have changed my mind about being with you, but I would have come into this with a different set of lenses, you know. We have talked to no end about what it's going to be like when you come home. We should have had a serious discussion about what would happen if you were flopped. I'm going to wait for as long as needed, but I didn't think about that possibility in the beginning. Baby, I look to you to be real with me, to prepare me for the worst, because you know this system better than I do. There's nothing wrong with being optimistic, but you've had me in La La Land all this time."

Shaka wrote back days later. "I feel like a complete ass for not giving you the worst-case scenario. Honestly, I am afraid to think of the worst case, but I know I have to for us. I don't want you to just be prepared for when I come home. You need to be prepared for if I don't."

On our next call, we discussed the worst case.

"Here's what I know. You're serving time for second degree murder. You have an assault on staff charge, for which you spent almost five years in the hole. This gives you two major assaultive charges, and in the last two years you've gotten two major misconducts. On the flip side, you pleaded out on all charges and took responsibility. You have made positive contributions to the captive population as well as built working relationships with the prison administration as a block rep and tutor. You have a job waiting for you at Malik's bookstore and the support of family and friends and the community. So what are the possibilities?"

"A deferral, where they would give me a parole pending completion of AOP, a flop for twelve months, and a flop for twenty-four months."

"Anything else?"

"Nah, that's it."

"What do we do if you get flopped?"

"There's really nothing we can do. There's no appeal process for parole decisions. We just have to wait for them to call me back again."

"And how long will that take?"

"It depends. Lately they been calling guys back early."

"I hate this fucking system!" I screamed. Every bone in

my body, every cell, hated everybody that had any part in the system—the police, the courts, the jails, the prisons. I hated them for tearing families apart. For making it so damn hard to stay connected. For locking up Black men at higher rates than any other group. For playing games with their freedom.

"I can do the time. If they gave me a twenty-four, it wouldn't stress me any more than it has. It would be hard to accept but I would continue to prepare myself for the day I am released. The hardest part is knowing how hurt you and my family would be."

I went online to the discussion forum and searched the Michigan Parole and Probation group. I sat up half the night reading the stories of women whose husband or son had seen the parole board, the interview went well, and they still got flopped. Some of those folks had braced themselves for the worst so they were disappointed but not crushed. Then there were others who were completely blindsided. I didn't want that to be me. I started preparing myself for the possibility that Shaka might not be coming home on September 26, 2008, his earliest release date.

I heard Mama's voice in my head, "You're a fool."

34

was still dealing with the reality that Shaka might not be getting paroled that year when I got a letter from him. He started, "This is by far the hardest letter I have ever had to write you." My heart fell to my stomach. I braced myself for what I was about to read. "It's hard because I hate to disappoint you. However, my actions today will do just that. Not only did I let you down, I let myself down." Shaka had decided to get one of his old tattoos covered up but got caught before the tattoo artist could finish. That's considered a major misconduct—accomplice to dangerous contraband, the tattoo gun. A major misconduct can result in a new case, time in the hole, or top lock, a sanction that confines the inmate to his cell except for meals. Shaka was given two weeks of top lock. That meant he couldn't use the phone or go out for recreation.

His letter continued, "I feel so stupid right now. I should have been more patient and waited until I came home or was in a more secure place. I am really sorry. I was being selfish and didn't weigh things out the way I should have. That was truly a lapse in judgment on my behalf. I don't make excuses for my actions. I know you are pissed at me and you have every right to be. I feel so lame even having to write you about this. I hope when you calm down that you will forgive me."

I put the letter down. I had spent hours trying to help Shaka prepare the best possible case to present to the board. Now what? He was about five months away from seeing the parole board. The odds were already stacked against him. He couldn't afford to take the kind of chances he'd taken early in his bid.

I moped around the house for days—part angry, part sad. Finally, once the anger subsided, I wrote him. "I have been too numb to write you the last few days. I got your letter. I was beyond disappointed. I felt like my world had come tumbling down around me. I was hurt, angry, frustrated, confused, saddened. I read your words over and over in disbelief. I've never felt so crushed. You know I've been on a roller coaster ride of emotions these last few weeks, but I've remained hopeful. Your news, however, just deflated my hopes."

Shaka wrote back, "The misconduct will not impact the parole board's decision one way or another."

I grew even more angered by his optimism. I couldn't type fast enough when I responded to his letter. "How in the hell do you know that? This is what I was talking about in my letter about you preparing me for the worst when it came to your parole board hearing. The reality is you don't know how this ticket is going to affect their decision, so why would you tell me that it won't? Are you trying to protect me? Or are you being optimistic for your own good? Now more than ever, we need to be focused on freedom. We're months away, literally, from you coming home and we just can't afford shit like this. That means taking no risks." I begged him, "Baby please, I can't handle the stress."

Shaka tried to explain why he'd gotten the tattoo. "Getting tattoos is a spiritual experience for me. The pain I endure reminds me of how hard life can be. But on the other side of that pain is the pleasure I get seeing my vision come to life." I didn't have any tattoos, but I tried to understand. "Baby, this is one of the few times I get to control what happens to my body," he continued. This I understood. There is freedom in choosing what happens to our body. I thought about being fifteen and choosing to lose my virginity. I thought about the choice I made, at nineteen, to cut all my hair off, then grow locs, then cut my hair again. The anger started melting away.

"I wasn't trying to minimize the impact of the ticket or protect you from reality. I was just telling you what I believe. I know there are no certainties when it comes to getting a parole, but I truly believe that they are going to give me a shot. If I didn't believe it, I would never tell you I did."

Shaka warned me that the department could take away some of the good time he'd earned, which would change his earliest release date. I checked OTIS every day and finally, after about a week, they updated his public record. I told Shaka when he called.

"They moved your ERD to October first."

"That's not bad. The last ticket I got they took ninety days. I'm looking at a deferral anyway since they haven't gotten me into AOP, so it may not make that much of a difference."

"I can't do this anymore," I interrupted, the weight of prison pressing on my mind.

"What do you mean?"

"These long trips up north. These high-ass phone bills. Just the thought of having to do this for another *minute* depresses me." It felt like every time we got close to the finish line, they moved it.

Shaka tried to make me feel better. "I feel so selfish."

"Why?"

"I have exposed you to a pain you would have never known had you not met me. And there is nothing I can do to take that pain away other than to come home. I don't know what to do. I can't change things. All I can do is continue to work toward freedom. All I know at this point is that we have what it takes to make it over any obstacle in our path. I remain full of faith and hope. No setback will change that."

"I'm not going anywhere," I sighed, settling into the reality of the life I'd chosen. "But this shit isn't easy."

35

Some days it felt like I was holding my breath. Holding my breath or holding a space for him in my life, I couldn't tell the difference. I missed museum exhibits. I turned down invites to concerts. I passed on the Essence Festival and the Roots Picnic. "I want us to experience those things together," Shaka told me. "I'll be home soon, and we'll get to do all that stuff and more."

I'd long dreamt about having a partner to share the things I loved. Art shows, films, festivals. I pictured romantic picnics at the park, dreamy dinners with idyllic views, travel to remote destinations. I pictured us standing on a balcony in some faraway paradise, the two of us hugged up and watching the sunset in dramatic pink, orange, and purple. I counted the ways we would pamper each other.

Whenever I saw Black couples, I'd think of me and Shaka. I'd imagine it was us holding hands walking through the mall or sitting in a crowded movie theater sharing popcorn. I got lost in the life we would one day share. A life far from concrete and steel and barbed wire.

I did everything I could to live a normal life and keep my mind off how long I had to wait. My work at the school and in the community kept me busy. Almost every night of the week I was at a meeting that ended later than scheduled, getting home too late and too tired to cook dinner. My Saturday mornings were spent in a community garden weeding and watering or tending the garden in my own yard. I pictured Shaka there with me, wherever I was. I thought about the conversations we'd have on the ride home, the love we'd make at the end of a long day. My life felt incomplete without Shaka there by my side.

In late March, Mama moved in with me. Arthritis in her knee and ankle made it difficult for her to work, and without a steady income, she lost her house, my childhood home on Marlowe.

"You won't regret this," she told me one day through tears as we packed up the house she'd called home for twenty-seven years. She'd bought the small ranch from the owner years earlier—the first house she'd purchased on her own.

I put my resentments aside. "You're my mother. I got you. My home is your home now."

Most mornings I woke up to the familiar smell of coffee and the sound of talk radio. Sometimes I'd come home to a cooked meal, a vegetarian recipe she'd found in a magazine, or discover she'd gone grocery shopping and picked up my favorite foods. We were like a married couple and I was the husband, coming home every evening to a clean house and dinner on the stove.

Mama's presence filled some of the empty spaces in my life

but none of it eased the sting of missing Shaka. Every Monday and Thursday I waited by the phone for him to call. Ojibway did transfers on Tuesdays and Fridays and Shaka always called the night before a transfer to let me know he'd be riding out. Those calls never came.

Shaka and I were about to celebrate our second anniversary when my brother suggested we do a family trip, our first vacation together since Daddy died. He was married with one child and one on the way, and since he lived in New Jersey, just outside of New York City, Mama and I hardly got to see him.

"That's a great idea. Mama would love that, but I don't know how I'm gonna be able to make that work right now. Things are kind of tight."

"I know, but our timeshare has two bedrooms and a kitchen. We can go grocery shopping when we get there and cook our own food. All you have to do is get your plane tickets and we got the rest."

A few days later, Shaka called. Guilt came as soon as I saw UNKNOWN on the caller ID. I didn't want to tell Shaka about the trip. We hadn't seen each other in six months. I desperately wanted to see him again, but I needed a break, a distraction from the longing.

"Hey baby," I said, trying to sound normal.

"Hey gorgeous. How was your day?"

"Good," I replied, debating in my mind whether to tell him now or later. "I talked to my brother the other day."

"Oh yeah? What's he up to?"

"Him and Krista are planning a trip to Orlando and he invited me and my mama to join them. He said all I have to do is get our plane tickets."

"That's what's up. When is he talking about going?"

I took a deep breath before responding. "Next month, the week of our anniversary." I waited for Shaka's disappointment. We hadn't been able to spend our first anniversary together, and now I'd be gone for our second.

"I know how important your family is to you. It's all good. Go and have a good time."

"Thank you for understanding, baby. It means a lot."

A week later when I bought me and Mama's plane tickets, the guilt was still there. It felt like I was leaving Shaka behind, celebrating our anniversary without him.

The Florida sun was just what I needed. For seven days I filled up on my brother's love and the smiles of my two-year-old niece Karly and forgot about AOP and the parole board and the unknown. I didn't write one letter or think about when I was going to make the ten-hour trek to Ojibway again.

36

n June, days after Shaka's thirty-sixth birthday, the books arrived. They were beautiful. I couldn't have been happier with the way everything turned out—the binding, the cover, the fonts, the formatting. I loved the way the book felt in my hand. I knew Shaka would fall in love. I rushed to the post office.

"Baby, I am so hyped right now. I got the book!" Shaka said, beaming through the phone. "You did an amazing job. I can't begin to tell you how much I appreciate you. You worked so hard on this. Thank you again for believing in me."

I was smiling so hard my cheeks hurt. "I'm so proud of you and the man you've become. It was a pleasure to work on this project. I'm excited about getting it out there. I know it takes time to really create a buzz, especially on a national level, but I'm going to do what I can to get it in the right hands. I can't wait to see you shine, baby. It's only a matter of time before you'll be out here doing your thing."

The arrival of the books gave us both a jolt of energy.

I started working on our website. I had no experience developing websites, but we didn't have the budget to hire a professional, so I used a template and figured out the rest on my own. Next up was driving traffic to the site.

Shaka went into straight hustle mode. It had been two years since that first conversation about publishing his work so he couldn't wait to get started. We talked about ways to penetrate the hip-hop market, the largest consumers of street lit. Hip-hop culture is an integral part of prison culture so Shaka suggested we send a copy of *Crack* to the rappers who were in prison at the time. Lil Wayne. T.I. Shyne. Remy Ma. "Their stamp of approval will mean everything in this environment," Shaka told me. He also suggested we try to secure a book review in all the leading hip-hop magazines—*FEDS, Black Men, Don Diva, XXL, The Source*—so I got busy researching the submission process for each publication.

Shaka was buzzing with ideas and wanted everything done *now*. "We can't let our foot off the pedal," he reminded me. If he asked me to do something and it wasn't done by the next time we talked, he got frustrated.

"A lot of times I feel you support me one hundred percent as my woman but eighty percent as my business partner. What I mean is there are things you have done or will do because as my woman you want to see me happy, but there are things that need to be done to make the business successful that I have to nag you about, and I wouldn't have to if you were thinking like a businesswoman one hundred percent of the time. This is why I get frustrated at times. I know how to separate the two, but I'm not sure that you do."

I felt like I was there for Shaka one hundred percent, period. I didn't have the time he had to focus exclusively on the business. I was juggling our relationship, our new business, a full-time job, and my work in the community. I loved being his rock, but I began to feel overwhelmed by his many requests. I did what I thought was my best, but it never seemed to be enough.

Shaka continued, "When it comes to business, I know I can be demanding. I feel an urgent need to get things done in a specific time frame. I am in foreign territory. I am close to freedom. I wish I could just relax and go with the flow, but I don't have that luxury. I watch these guys squander their time away and it is frustrating. But their reality is different from mine. It's a lot easier to start over after two years than it is to start over after seventeen years. Some nights I lay awake for hours thinking about how things are going to be when I get out. Sometimes it is frightening and a little overwhelming to think about. You're going to have to be patient with me."

"There isn't anything I wouldn't do for you, you know that. I understand the sense of urgency you feel, and trust me, I'm committed to helping you make your dream a reality before you come home, but you have to be patient with me too. I'm doing this all alone."

Shaka wanted to move the books in bulk rather than focus on individual sales. He suggested we create a street team. Friends and family would buy copies of the book from us at a discounted price and then sell them at the retail price.

"I have a couple of guys who say they want to get their

people to get some books, so they can spread the word and make a couple of dollars. I'll connect them with you once I hear back."

"Sounds good. So how much are you thinking we'd sell the books to the street team for?"

"Five dollars. That means they'd make ten dollars on each sale."

"That's too low. The industry standard is forty percent off the retail price. That would be nine dollars per book. We'd be able to recoup our expenses faster."

Shaka was thinking of his experience in the streets. He broke it down for me. "When I was in the streets, we had this saying that good dope sold itself. The most important thing in business is maintaining credibility when it comes to your product. Once word spreads that you lack a quality product, people hesitate to do business with you. And we never liked to hold our product for too long because the longer you hold on to it, the more money you lose because your spending outpaces your income. So instead of trying to make a four- or five-thousand-dollar profit in the long run by cutting our rocks smaller, we opted to cut ours bigger and move them faster. The more hands we get the books in, the faster we build our brand."

"Hmmm, I see what you're saying. Let's see how it goes."

Shaka got busy setting up deals with his friends and family to sell the books in bulk and I worked on a marketing and distribution plan. Right away I learned about the Harlem Book Fair, the largest Black book fair in the country. The vending fees were more than I could afford but I decided to go to get a feel for the event.

West 135th Street was packed from curb to curb with faces in every shade of brown. The Harlem sun beat down on my neck as I weaved in and out of the crowd, browsing books and picking up promo materials. I studied the book displays and watched how authors engaged passersby. Some authors brought a team who passed out postcards or bookmarks or walked into the crowd to invite people to their table. Others just stood behind their table and smiled. About half of the vendors were independent booksellers like us who had gone the self-publishing route, a growing trend in publishing. I saw names I recognized and brands that had defined the genre of street lit, or urban lit as it's also called. I was bursting with excitement by the end of the day. I couldn't wait to fill Shaka in.

When I returned to Detroit, I turned my attention to book clubs and online book reviewers like the African American Literature Book Club (AALBC) and Urban Book Source, the go-to website for all things street lit. I sent review copies to both and then waited. I checked their websites religiously, and finally, after six months, our first review was posted.

"Motion picture action, detailed description is what happens when traveling through the gritty streets of Detroit while reading *Crack Volume 1*," the review started.

I read it to Shaka when he called.

"Damnnn!" he said, pausing to let it soak in. His only audience had been the guys in prison who'd read his tattered unbound manuscripts. The review was confirmation—he was on the right path. "We about to change the game, baby."

His to-do lists for me got longer, and my patience grew shorter.

One day I lost it. "Then don't ask me to do nothing else for you," I shouted through the phone, tired of him complaining about what I hadn't done.

The phone grew quiet. Shaka let my words sit there in the silence.

And then he spoke. "That's how you feel? You know it's never been easy for me to ask other people to do things for me. I've never felt like anyone had my back one hundred percent the way I had theirs. It's always been easier for me to make my own way. Then I met you. From the very beginning I felt like you were a woman I could share everything with. And I saw you as a partner in every sense of the word. You are the only person who I can count on to have my back."

His words disarmed me. "I'm sorry, baby. I know it's hard for you to be dependent on others. You know I got your back."

"I rely on you to handle basically everything, so your words really cut deep. I don't know what to say. I think I'm going to need some time to think through this."

"What do you mean?" I asked, confused.

"To hear that coming from you hit me really hard. When it comes to trusting someone else to be your eyes and ears and hands, there is a power dynamic created. It felt like you were making a power play in order to win the argument. The first thing I thought about is, what will happen when we're at home arguing and you feel like you aren't winning? Are you going to remind me that it's your house and if I don't like it, I can move out? I mean, how far are you willing to go in order to win?"

"This isn't about winning, Shaka. I'm just tired. I'm tired of doing this alone. I didn't mean to hurt you. I know it was immature, but don't you think you're taking this to the extreme?"

"You might see it as just a smartass comment, but I think there's something deeper there. I don't think we should have our call on Wednesday," he announced with finality. "I just need some space to think."

I was speechless.

Shaka didn't even say I love you before he hung up the phone.

I thought we had an understanding—never get off the phone angry. It might take a few weeks to resolve an argument because our communication was so limited, but we'd never shut each other out. That night, our communication broke down completely. Our separate stresses about getting him into AOP, about securing his life on the outside seemed to be getting to us.

"I'll be here when you're ready to talk," I wrote in a letter as soon as we got off the phone.

Lying in the bed that night, I felt more alone than I'd felt in the two years we'd been together. We only talked on the phone twice a week and he had taken away the one thing that made the distance bearable.

The silence was painful. Time slowed down again.

I was surprised when I saw UNKNOWN on my caller ID on Wednesday.

"Hey," I answered, unsure what to expect on the other end.

"Hey."

"I didn't think I was going to hear from you tonight."

"You knew I was going to call you."

"No, I didn't. We've never gotten off the phone like that. You didn't even say I love you."

"I just wasn't feeling it. I couldn't even mouth the words

I love you. I know you think I am overreacting but at the root of all of this is trust. How can I trust you to have my back after something like that?"

"Shaka, I want to be that rock you can depend on, but honestly, life sometimes gets so busy that I can't make things happen for you when you may want or need. Sometimes I feel like you're not sensitive to what might be going on in my life. Like I may have spent my evening at a meeting and didn't get home until after nine o'clock. When I come home, I just want to chill. I don't want to think. I just sat up in a meeting for two to three hours thinking."

"The last thing I want to be is a burden to you."

"You're not a burden. Sometimes it's your tone. Your tone suggests I'm not handling my business or I'm neglecting you, and depending on what my day might have been like, I take that personally. It makes me feel like my sacrifices aren't enough."

"I'm sorry if it comes across that way. You know I appreciate everything you do. I'm just a very direct person and I have no problem asking for what I want or speaking up if I feel my needs aren't being met. Outside of our relationship, this company is the only thing that makes me happy. It gives me hope and keeps me going on those days when I don't even want to get out of bed. It's tangible evidence of my transformation and I want to see it succeed."

We talked for close to an hour. I was emotionally drained by the end of the call. He said he understood. I said I understood. But we'd always end up in the same place, feeling unheard.

stood in the shower crying. The tears rolled down my face easy, helped along by the steam. I'd called Lansing again. There's a group starting at Ojibway in two weeks, the man on the other end told me. He'll be in that class. I wanted to curse him, but I said nothing.

It was July and I'd been told in February that Shaka would be transferred within sixty days to take AOP. When that didn't happen, they made more promises. "There's a class starting next week. I'll call you back to confirm he's in that class." I never got that call.

I'd gotten my hopes up that Shaka would be moved closer to home to take AOP but now he'd be taking the class at Ojibway. That meant ten more months up north.

I broke down again as I drove to work. A lonely tear slid down my cheek, and then another and another until tears rushed down my face. The longing, the loneliness, all of the unknowns came crashing down on me at once. I wanted to scream but instead I sobbed, the tears releasing months of frustration.

That night, I wrote Shaka. "I'm trying to see the bright side of all this. I've been praying for God's will to be done, and I trust that this is in God's will. It might not make sense to us right now, but it will in due time. I've surrendered this whole situation to the Creator, so I trust that your class will go well and finish on schedule and you'll get an excellent report from the psych."

Two weeks later, a day before the group was set to start, the class was canceled. We were back at square one.

Shaka saw the parole board the next month. His interview didn't go well. There was nothing we could do but grumble to each other about how unfair the system is. No one would care that the parole board member who interviewed him was rude and antagonistic, cutting him off repeatedly.

"Mr. White, you killed a man over nothing," she said coldly.

"I felt threatened," Shaka tried to explain.

"That's a weak excuse, Mr. White." She did most of the talking. She didn't care about the man Shaka had become. She focused on the crime he'd committed, on the nineteen-year-old who'd taken a man's life. "I am recommending you take AOP," she said, and then ended the interview.

We felt helpless.

Three weeks later, I watched the film *The Secret*. It was exactly what I needed when I needed it. I'd had the DVD in the bottom of my purse for months but one night, in my boredom, I decided to see what the hype was about. I was familiar with the precepts of the law of attraction through my study of

The Kybalion, a book of ancient Egyptian teachings that explain the seven principles or laws of the Universe—the principle of mentalism, the principle of correspondence, the principle of vibration, the principle of polarity, the principle of rhythm, the principle of cause and effect, and the principle of gender. These principles are said to be the foundation of wisdom and speak to the connectedness of all things. Watching these ideas come to life in *The Secret* was a reminder of how powerful the mind is. *Our thoughts create our reality.*

Right away, I went to work applying *The Secret*. I started with gratitude, writing down everything I was grateful for. The usual—my health, my family, a beautiful home. I thought about the experiences I wanted to have and how I wanted to feel. I wrote statements in the present tense as though these things were already *present* in my life. I am at peace, I wrote. Shaka is home. I am a mommy to three beautiful and healthy children. Shaka and I travel the world together. I am surrounded by good people who are encouraging and uplifting. I work for the benefit of my family and bring sufficient money into our household to live abundantly. I have time to volunteer for the causes I believe in.

I posted sticky notes with these affirmations in as many places as possible—on my dashboard, on my dresser mirror, on my desk at work—as daily reminders of what I wanted to manifest in my life. This exercise helped shift my thoughts. It kept me focused on the good I wanted to attract instead of the pain and frustration of our circumstances.

For the law of attraction to work, according to the film, you must surrender and trust that what you want is on its way. So

I surrendered. I stopped calling Lansing. I stopped calling the warden. I stopped trying to fix it.

Within weeks, I got the call. "I'm riding out tomorrow, baby," Shaka announced, his voice filled with relief and excitement. He was finally getting transferred after sixteen months at Ojibway and more than two years up north. I found comfort knowing he couldn't be sent farther away—Ojibway was in the northernmost corner of the state. When I got the call that he'd landed at Harrison Correctional Facility in Adrian, which is only an hour from Detroit, I got on the road.

Hope returned.

38

Adrian was close enough for me to visit once a week, sometimes more. We talked for hours about everything and nothing, and when we tired of talking we'd just sit and people-watch. When we pulled out the Scrabble board, the no-holds-barred competitor in us came out.

"Ha! Thirty-six points," I teased as I counted the last tile on the board.

"Not bad."

"Not bad? That's better than you did."

"I'm just getting warmed up." Shaka laughed. "This is what I do."

In the crowded room, we laughed as though we were the only ones there. "So what you saying? You smarter than me?"

"Well," he said, smiling.

It felt as if we had gone back in time to those first days visiting at Cooper Street, but now we were closer to freedom.

In what was typically an eight-hour visit, we'd eat two meals together—lunch and dinner. I relaxed my dietary restrictions for those treasured hours, eating the only vegetarian-friendly food in the vending machines—Fritos, Lay's Plain Chips, the occasional wilted salad with iceberg lettuce, Raisinettes, and Reese's Peanut Butter Cups. The food was overpriced, but it was better than the food Shaka got in the chow hall. Most days he chose either a sliced turkey sandwich with barbeque sauce or roast beef with mustard. Sometimes there was cheese pizza for me. I cringed with every bite. Not only was the cheese not organic, God only knows what they put in it trying to make the pizza for as little as possible to sell it for as much as possible to people who didn't have much of a choice.

With weekly visits, our connection was rekindled. When we weren't eating or playing Scrabble, we were touching each other in some way—our arms linked together, his arm around my shoulders, my leg leaning against his. The moment our hands touched, our palms warm and sweaty, it seemed every cell in my body came alive. When it was time for goodbyes, we kissed for as long as they'd allow, our tongues moving deliberately, leaving an imprint in our mouths until we kissed again.

The hardest part of our visits was always the last goodbye. I could feel Shaka watching me as I walked out of the visiting room and through the Plexiglas door, his eyes willing me not to go. I'd turn around and meet his gaze once I walked through the door, smiling one last time before another set of doors opened and the day's visitors were set free.

Shaka had been in Adrian about a month when we got word that his parole had been denied. We weren't surprised. He hadn't finished AOP. I reminded him of the divine order of the Universe, but this time Shaka was the one who didn't want to hear the optimism.

"You will never understand what it is taking for me to remain hopeful and optimistic," he wrote. "I have given myself more self-talks than you can imagine and after a while it gets to be too much. I know your heart is in the right place and you mean well."

"I know it's not easy to keep bouncing back one setback after the other. But this too shall pass, my love," I wrote him, still trying to be encouraging. "Just know that I am here for you and with you through this storm and the next one and the next one."

discovered a winter storm was headed our way as I got dressed for my visit one Saturday morning. I didn't think much of it. I knew how to drive in snow. It's the ice that scares me, and, after all, Shaka was only an hour's drive away. Snow or no snow, I thought, I'll be fine. I headed out around 11am hoping to beat the storm.

About 30 miles into my drive, I saw one vehicle, then two vehicles spin out on the highway. I slowed down. The snow crunched beneath the weight of my tires as I crept along. When I saw my exit, I sighed. *Finally*. I still had 30 more miles, but the worst was behind me, I thought.

Ten minutes later, I started to panic. The snow had made it hard to see where the road ended and the cornfields on both sides began. Two hours into what was usually an hour drive, I drove into a ditch.

I couldn't get reception on my cell phone, so I sat for a couple minutes thinking of my options. Everything around me was covered in snow. I looked ahead, and then behind me, hoping to see another car driving down the two-lane road, or maybe someone in one of the farmhouses I'd just passed saw me ride into the ditch.

After waiting ten full minutes for someone to see me stranded on the side of the road, I decided to walk for help. I estimated that the house behind me was closer than the house ahead of me. When my boots hit the ground, I remembered I'd worn my dressy black boots with a three-inch heel. I tiptoed through the snow holding my head halfway down to shield my eyes against the snowflakes.

The flakes fell quickly. I couldn't see more than a few inches ahead of me. When I reached the closest house, I did not see any signs of life. There was no car in the driveway, no lights on inside, nothing. It was eerily quiet. I approached the steps, nervous. I was in a rural white town and I'm sure they didn't see many Black faces. I took a deep breath and knocked. No answer. I knocked again. Still no answer.

What do I do now? The other house was even farther away. I'd barely made it to the first house without falling and now my feet were cold and wet.

I zipped my coat as far as it would go, tightened the short collar around my neck, and tiptoed back to my car. I sat in silence for a few minutes, and then remembered I had an old bag of cat litter in the trunk. I'd read cat litter gives your wheels traction, so I kept a bag for emergencies. I climbed out of the car, opened the trunk, and grabbed the unused bag of litter. I tore it open and poured some on the snow, just behind my two back tires.

When I started the car again and tried to drive, the wheels started spinning. I could hear the tiny pebble-like grains of the cat litter slapping against my tires. I stopped, took a deep breath, and then pressed my foot into the gas pedal again. It wasn't working. I got out and poured more cat litter under the tires. I pressed the pedal as far into the floor of my Saturn as it would go and rocked with as much force as I could create. I revved the engine and tried to build momentum. I felt the front tires move. Hopeful, I kept rocking, flooring the gas pedal with each push forward. Suddenly, the whole car started moving. "Yes!" I screamed.

I didn't take my foot off the gas as I guided the car back to the dusty road now completely covered in a fresh blanket of pearly white snow. I put both hands on the steering wheel, at three o'clock and nine o'clock, my eyes looking straight ahead. The small car strained to move through the dense snow. I inched along, trying not to stop, trying not to veer too far left or too far right. It felt like I was driving through thick, heavy cement as it dried.

I'd driven about 50 yards when my car finally stopped. I had approached an intersection where I needed to make a slight right turn, and then a left turn, but the snow was too high and too heavy for my wheels to turn or move any farther. There I was, alone, stuck in the intersection. And still no sign of life. The sky was gray now turning to black as the winter sun started to set. The snow sparkled against the darkness.

I looked out of the window hopelessly. I had no idea how I was going to get myself out of this trouble. I turned off the ignition.

Then, out of nowhere, I saw a huge snowplow barreling down the road, coming toward me. I couldn't get out of my car—the snow was so high my door wouldn't open—so I said a quick prayer, hoping the driver would see me.

The plow stopped just a few feet in front of me. The driver

jumped down from the truck and grabbed a shovel off the back. I watched with nervous anticipation as he threw snow in every direction trying to get me unstuck. Then finally, freedom. I thanked him profusely.

"No problem," he replied. "Have a good night, ma'am. And be careful."

Fortunately, I was headed in the direction he'd just plowed.

My hands trembled as I drove the last 15 miles to the prison. My mind was all over the place. I kept thinking of what could have happened.

I eased into the parking lot, the sky now completely black. The snow had stopped, and the lot had been cleared. There were ten or so cars there, unusual for a Saturday, the busiest visiting day of the week. I rushed into the building, scribbled my name and Shaka's in the visitors book, and went straight to the restroom. I tried to shake off the tension in my neck and shoulders, but I couldn't. I put on some lip gloss and pretended to be okay. I'd only been waiting about 5 minutes when the officer called me up to be processed. I went through the motions as she searched my body for contraband. After countless searches, my skin is indifferent to the weight of her touch.

I couldn't wait to see Shaka. I was hours late for our visit and I knew he was worried. The minute I reached the visiting room and saw his face, I broke down in tears. I fell into his arms and hugged him tighter than I'd ever hugged him before.

About a month later, on a typical Saturday visit, I noticed something different about Shaka's arms.

"Are you serious?" I asked, my eyes staring sharply at Shaka.

The lines on a couple of his tattoos looked darker, the black ink more visible against his brown skin. I couldn't believe my eyes.

"What?" he asked innocently, his eyes convicting him.

"You know what I'm talking about," I replied, looking down at his arm. "Don't tell me you got more work done." I wanted to go home, crawl into my bed, and sleep until it was all over.

Shaka looked at me and cracked a half-smile, hoping to lighten the mood. "I just had him redo the lines on a couple of my tattoos," he said matter-of-factly.

"What if you had gotten caught? I can't believe you'd take that risk again."

"Listen, I didn't get caught. Calm down."

I was furious. "Sometimes I wonder if you really understand how scary this has been for me. I get that we both have different comfort levels when it comes to risk, but c'mon. You said you were going to wait until you got home to get any more work done."

I didn't want to spend the day going back and forth so I let it go. We couldn't afford to waste one visit.

Later, I wrote him. "Baby, I try to understand what's shaped your life and why you do what you do, but the reality is I've never spent a day in prison. I would never try to compare what you experience in there with what I experience out here, but I just want you to put yourself in my shoes for a minute. It's not easy to be out here without you, but I make the sacrifices I need to make because I love you and I believe in you. I'm just asking you to make this one sacrifice for me. We're almost at the finish line."

I hated it when we were at odds with each other, but I knew our ability to communicate, to recover from arguments would serve us well once he was on the outside.

40

As spring approached, we got word that the parole board wanted to see Shaka again, three months earlier than scheduled. Early callbacks are a good sign, plus the chances of parole increase significantly with the second interview, so we were excited. Shaka grew restless as the day approached.

"My every hope and dream is wrapped up in one interview," he wrote in a letter I got the week before his hearing. "I can't sleep at night or think straight during the day because I know how much this day means to me, to us."

I was as anxious as he was, but I reassured him when I wrote him back, "Everything's going to be fine. You're done with AOP now and you got a good report. They have all your support letters and your certificates. You got this."

His hearing was held on our anniversary, another good sign, we thought. It was a beautiful spring day. The sun was beaming with not a cloud in sight. Shaka had no idea what time they'd call him for his interview, so I kept my phone close by, eager for him to call and tell me how things had gone. I could barely focus at work waiting on my phone to ring.

I smiled from ear to ear when I finally saw UNKNOWN pop up on my cell phone. I stepped outside for some privacy.

"Hey, baby!" I sang.

"Hey, gorgeous. What's good?"

"Don't play. Now you know I've been waiting all morning for you to call."

"I know," he laughed. I listened as Shaka ran the whole morning down to me—before, during, and after the interview. He knew how much I liked details.

"I waited in the hallway on this bench with a couple other guys seeing the board."

"Was your father able to wait there with you?"

"Yeah, but we didn't really talk to each other."

"Was your counselor there?"

"Yeah, he was there."

"Cool. Were you nervous?"

"Baby, when they called my name, my heart dropped to my stomach."

This time the interview went well. Shaka was interviewed by a different board member, another woman, but she allowed him to speak without interruption. She listened to him describe what happened that fateful night and asked him questions about the changes he'd made in his life.

"She seemed impressed with the work I've done. This is it, baby. I'm coming home. I can feel it," Shaka said, beaming.

"I feel it too." I couldn't stop smiling.

We said every year was going to be our year, but we felt the stars were finally lining up in our favor.

Waiting for their decision felt like torture. Nothing was guaranteed. Parole boards can be unpredictable. We tried not to talk about it—the decision or our feelings—but it always felt like the elephant in the room. We did what we could to keep each other's spirits lifted. Letters were our love language.

"You are a dynamic brother and I am amazed at the strength you exhibit even in your most vulnerable moments. You are my King, and I stand proudly alongside you as your Queen. It is only a matter of days before we hear the good news and we'll soon be able to share the throne together as husband and wife. Trust!"

"As much as I want to come home, I think I want to say the words 'Baby, I am coming home' even more. I know that sounds crazy, but your happiness means the world to me. Just the thought of hearing you scream in excitement makes my heart flutter. I have that moment etched in my mind more than any other. You are a true ridah of a woman and it is your time to shine. That moment is near, and I know it is only a matter of time before I will be able to make that call we have both been dreaming and longing for."

I was so excited I started preparing for Shaka's homecoming. I shopped for some of the things he'd need and some new things for the house. Shopping kept me from sitting at home, letting the anxiety build. I wanted to buy all new everything—new pillows, new towels, new rugs, new dishes—to mark our new beginning, but my pockets said, "Slow down."

Then, finally, after three weeks, I got the call.

"They gave me a flop," Shaka said through clenched teeth, sadness rising in his voice. He was a "menace to society," they claimed. The parole board has absolute discretion to decide whether an inmate should be released. There are ten board members, but a three-member panel makes the decision. Shaka needed two of the three panel members to vote yes, but the two who hadn't interviewed him, who'd only looked at his file, voted no.

"Baby, nooo!" I broke down crying. The phone grew silent, then I said, "I'm on my way." We needed each other in that moment, the gravity of the news weighing more than our words could carry.

41

My mind was all over the place as I walked into the visiting room. Shaka was waiting along the wall, seated with the other guys anticipating visitors. When our eyes met, we forced a smile. He stood, and we embraced with the full force of our bodies. I wished we could stand there holding each other, suspended in that moment, but the officers didn't care that he'd just heard the most devastating news, that he *needed* my embrace.

We walked hand in hand to our seats, an electrical current crisscrossing back and forth from his hand to mine and mine to his. I could feel the tears beginning to well up in my eyes as we sat down. Then, the tears flowed—his and mine. It was only the second time I'd seen him cry, and the second time he'd cried since he'd been in prison. Shaka looked into my eyes, his voice shaking, and said with finality, "I can't let you do this anymore. Not a day goes by that I don't think about what it must be like for you. You've been here for me through all this madness and I am forever grateful, but I can't see you suffer anymore." He struggled through the words, tears streaking his face. I listened to all the reasons why I should move on. Then he declared, "I'm done playing their game. I'm not going to see the parole board again."

I interrupted him. "There is no way in hell you are giving up and letting them win." I reached for his hands. "We are in it to win it, remember. I will never give up on you. Giving up is not an option, Shaka." I reminded him how strong he'd been to endure eighteen years of hell on earth. He squeezed my hands and gazed into my eyes, taking in every word.

"Thank you, baby. This is why I love you. It is extremely difficult to remain hopeful and optimistic, but your man is a fighter. I will never be counted amongst those who gave up or gave in to the system."

42

We waited again for Shaka to be called back to see the parole board. Though he had been given another 12-month continuance, which meant that the board would not consider his parole for another year, there was a good chance they would review his file sooner. The country was in the middle of the Great Recession and every department in the state was forced to make cuts. For the Department of Corrections, that meant closing prisons, laying off staff, and releasing more inmates. We hoped Shaka would benefit from the State's financial crisis.

"I have nothing to look forward to," Shaka wrote me one day. Some days it felt that way, but I knew if we wanted to manifest his freedom, we couldn't focus on what we didn't have. We had to focus on what we *did*. I suggested we write letters to the Creator and speak our intentions into the Universe.

"Between the two of us, I know we can create the energy needed to bring you home," I told him. "I think our collective energy is what got you transferred to Adrian last year and it will be what creates the conditions for you to be released."

"I'm with it, baby. Whatever you think will help. I'm still growing into my spiritual self and you have been good at nourishing that part of me. I'll admit, my mind wanders sometimes when it comes to the visualization stuff, especially in the morning because of all the movement around me, but I will continue to work on it and find ways to meditate and visualize everything we've dreamed of."

I opened up my laptop and started writing.

Dear Creator, Mother/Father God,

Thank you! Thank you! Thank you! Thank you for your love, your divine goodness, your grace, your guidance, your understanding, your forgiveness, your covering, your blessings, your light. Thank you for helping me to see the beauty in all things. Thank you for showing me how to love and how to receive love. Thank you for hearing my prayers and healing my soul. Thank you for revealing to me the power of acceptance. Thank you for helping me to see the big picture when things don't go my way. Thank you for inspiring me. Thank you for giving me the courage and the strength to weather life's many storms.

I am at peace right now because I know everything is as it should be. I trust that you will carry me and Shaka through this bumpy road in our journey together and keep us grounded in our love for you and each other. I trust that you have already prepared a way for us and it

*will all unfold in due time. I trust that our needs will be
met and our desires will be realized. I trust in the divine
order of the Universe and the universal law of attraction.
I commit to thinking positively and living righteously
so that I will attract all the goodness and beauty that is
mine.*

*It is my desire to have Shaka free and home with me
by December 31, 2009. I pray that the work he has done
to atone for the crimes he committed will be evident to
the parole board and he will be granted a parole. I pray
that his release is smooth and without complication. I
pray that he is assigned to a parole agent who is understanding, compassionate, and wants to see him succeed.
I pray that he is given few parole restrictions, which will
allow him to live as freely and comfortably as possible.
I trust that his release is in divine order and he will be
home soon . . .*

I wrote for a full hour. One page turned into four, and by
the time I finished, all the frustration had fallen away and hope,
once again, returned.

43

Eventually my friends and family got used to the idea of me being with Shaka and started asking, "When is he coming home?" I didn't know, which made that question more and more painful to hear. Shaka and I tried not to talk about it. What more could we say that hadn't already been said? I miss you. I love you. I need you.

I continued to visit every week. Visiting made the pain more bearable. We could lose ourselves in the moment, distracted from the ache in our hearts.

By the fall, Shaka had been transferred again, this time back to Cooper Street, where our relationship had blossomed three years earlier. I was headed to see him on a Friday afternoon, miles away from my exit, when I heard something pop under my hood. I was going at least 75mph in the left lane, and suddenly my car started decelerating. There was no room on the left shoulder, so I moved quickly from the left lane to the right shoulder and stopped the car. It was December, cold, and I was on the highway alone again.

A passerby stopped moments after I pulled onto the shoulder. I got out of my car as he approached.

"You want me to take a look under your hood?" he offered.

"Yes, thank you. I don't know a thing about cars."

He took a quick look and gave me the bad news. "Looks like something's wrong with your engine. You need a ride?" he asked me.

I sighed. "No, I'm good, thanks. I've got AAA." I thought about the snowstorm I'd barely survived. I was grateful I wasn't on one of those country roads again, stranded in the middle of nowhere.

"Well, be safe," he replied, then returned to his car.

I watched as he drove off, the traffic whizzing by me like race cars on a speedway. I climbed back in my car and started searching my purse for my AAA card.

"Where are you?" the dispatcher asked after a long wait.

"I'm not sure. I'm on I-94 West headed to Jackson." I tried my best to describe where I was, but my car had stopped in between mile markers and I was too far from the nearest exit to know which exit number was ahead of me.

The night descended on me as I waited in my car for the tow truck to arrive. Eventually Shaka called. I hadn't shown up for our visit.

"What's wrong, gorgeous?"

I told him what happened. He promised to call me again in fifteen minutes.

"Has the tow truck arrived?"

"No, not yet."

"You good?"

"Yeah. I'm just a little cold. The temperature's starting to drop."

About a half hour later, I saw the tow truck approaching me from my rearview mirror. The driver quickly hitched my car, then drove me to the nearest body shop. It was dark at this point and the shop was about to close, but the mechanic agreed to look at my car. I waited in the lobby. I felt vulnerable as a woman alone in a desolate town at night in a body shop filled with men. Correction, a *Black* woman alone in a small *white* town at night in a body shop filled with men.

Fifteen minutes later, the mechanic invited me into the garage and told me matter-of-factly, "You got a hole in your engine." How did that happen? I wondered. I'd driven up and down the highway for three years, including seven trips up north, and I'd only gotten my car serviced at the Saturn dealership. I asked the mechanic what it would cost to replace my engine. He pulled out the mechanic's bible and thumbed through a few pages. The price was $3,000 if I wanted a new engine and slightly less for a refurbished one. I told him I'd think about it. "You want the number to Enterprise?" he asked as he started locking up the shop.

Shaka called again on my way to pick up a rental car.

"What did they say about your car?"

"There's a hole in the engine."

"Damn, for real?"

"Yeah, the mechanic said it's going to be about three thousand dollars for a new engine. They were about to close so there's nothing I can do about it right now. I'm going to leave my car there and figure it out tomorrow. I'm on my way to Enterprise now to rent a car."

"Damn, I hate to hear this baby. I wish there was something I could do."

Shaka kept me calm through the whole ordeal. Once I rented the car, I drove down the road to the prison. I was only ten minutes away and there were still a couple hours before visiting hours ended.

During the recession, most Americans were one paycheck away from poverty if not steeped in it. The situation with my car was a major setback, especially because two months earlier I'd lost my job at the school. Nsoroma had to make some budget cuts and I was laid off. I couldn't afford to get a new engine or buy a new car. My mama, who'd gotten back on her feet and moved into a one-bedroom apartment not far from me, volunteered to take me grocery shopping or run errands whenever I needed. But I didn't dare ask her to drive me 80 miles to see Shaka.

I'd been fortunate. I hadn't had to rely on one of the van companies that take women like me to prisons every week. I could come and go when I wanted. Now I had to figure out how we were going to see each other.

Nothing seemed to be going right in my life. I had no idea when Shaka was coming home, no job, and now no car. Then one cold January day while I was in the library, I stumbled upon *The Key*, a book written by Joe Vitale, one of the gurus featured in *The Secret*. The book featured exercises to help the reader work through what Vitale called "limiting beliefs." I needed to clear whatever was blocking me from attracting what I wanted—Shaka's freedom.

The most powerful exercise I did asked me to write down what I was unhappy about. I thought about our circumstances. "I am tired of waiting, I am tired of trying to be strong for him and for me, I'm tired of being alone at night." Then Vitale asked two simple questions. Why are you unhappy about that? What would happen if you were *not* unhappy about that? I wrote in my journal, "For once in my life I have found a man who loves and adores me, and I can't be with him. I fear if this relationship doesn't work out, I'll never find another man like him and I'll be alone for the rest of my life."

I was afraid of losing the one man who'd loved me back. That fear, according to Vitale, was blocking me from attracting what I wanted.

"No one else will ever love me" was my limiting belief. To erase that thought, I wrote contrasting affirmations. "Love is abundant." "There are no limits to the goodness of the Universe." "I will find love with someone else if this relationship does not work out." I'd bought into the idea that Shaka was *the one*, so I clung desperately to him and put my happiness on layaway waiting for him to come home. Acknowledging the possibility that I could be happy by myself, or even with someone else, released the feelings of desperation. I didn't want to think about not being with Shaka, but I had to. I said to myself over and over, "My happiness does not depend on whether he's home." I found meaning again in my work in the community and I went out with friends whenever I could.

The minute I surrendered and decided to be happy with my *right now*, it felt as if a huge weight had been lifted. The anxiety fell away. I still missed Shaka. I still wanted him home. But I was no longer consumed with the outcome.

About two months later, Shaka got called back early to see the parole board. The interview went well again. This time he was interviewed by a man, a pastor from Benton Harbor. It was hard to get excited—the Department had played with our emotions one too many times—but we remained optimistic.

We were prepared for a long wait but just a couple weeks after Shaka's hearing, he called with the news.

"Baby, I'm coming home!" he shouted into the phone as soon as I answered.

"Babyyy! Oh my God. Are you serious?"

"Yeah, the counselor just gave me the news. It's official. This shit is finally about to be over."

We talked and laughed for what felt like hours, our voices free from the weight of prison. When we hung up the phone, I whispered, *Thank you.*

Shaka was transferred to Mound Correctional Facility in Detroit the next week. He'd serve his last sixty days there. I had driven by Mound many times before but never paid much attention. Mound is one of the two prisons in Detroit and shares a barbed wire fence with neighboring Ryan Correctional Facility.

Shaka was allowed eight visits a month and I didn't miss one. We spent most of our time talking about his homecoming and the life waiting for him on the other side. We were happy that he wouldn't have a curfew, but he couldn't leave the state. That was reasonable, but most parole restrictions aren't. They are designed for inmates to fail. In Michigan, parolees aren't allowed to associate with anyone who has a felony. That's damn near impossible if you're from the hood, where the rates of incarceration are highest. Parolees also can't be in a place that serves alcohol. Technically, that includes restaurants. Two-thirds of those released will return to prison within three years, most due to parole violations, not new crimes. We were determined Shaka was not going to be one of them.

On one of my visits, I told Shaka about some of the homecoming stories I'd read in the online discussion forum. Some guys, especially those who had served long sentences like Shaka, had a hard time adjusting to life on the outside. I wanted us to talk through what his experience might look like, but he was offended. He thought I was doubting him. He was different, he reminded me.

"I may have been in prison for nineteen years, but prison hasn't been in me. I'm not other guys. I did my bid differently. I have a vision for my life and how I want to live it and I don't want to be boxed in," he explained.

I told him I didn't want him to feel boxed in either. "Baby, trust me, I want you to soar to the heights of your potential. I know you're not trying to have anybody holding your hand when you come home but this is all new to me. I know every guy's experience is different, but there are similarities, like not wanting to be in large crowds or having people in your personal space. All I was trying to do was prepare myself for those kinds of things. I don't want to be naïve about your needs nor do I want to take things for granted."

"Gorgeous, I appreciate you trying to make my transition home as comfortable as possible. But you have to understand, a lot of guys coming home squandered their time away while they were in here. I've worked hard to earn my freedom and I'm ready to enjoy every moment of it."

"I hear you."

"But if I'm keeping it real, there is a part of me that's afraid."

I asked him what he was afraid of.

"I'm afraid of failing and letting everyone down. There are so many people counting on me to be that person they can look to with pride, you know. I've got you, my children, my parents, and then there's the hundreds of brothers in here counting on me to make it," he confessed.

"That's a lot of pressure. But you don't have anything to prove to me," I assured him. "No matter what happens, I will not be disappointed or discouraged. If you never face any of the emotional adjustments that other guys face, that's wonderful. Can either of us be certain that you won't? I don't think so. Yes, you are a different kind of man and everything that makes you who you are is what made me grow in love with you, but neither of us knows for certain what those first few weeks and months will be like."

"I know the initial adjustment period may be a bit of a challenge, but I'm good. It's not you I'm worried about. I know there are people out there who question whether I will be the man you need, and they'll be watching and waiting to see the cracks in our relationship. But, baby, I promise you, I won't let you down or fail you. This is the first time in my life where I've set out to do everything right and sometimes the thought of that causes me anxiety, but I'm ready."

"I'm ready, too. I just want you to know that you have a soft place to land with me. I want you to feel safe discussing whatever's on your mind, whatever you might be feeling, without fear that I'm going to try and box you in. I think an important part of a person's healthy transition from prison to home is discussing their feelings and sharing their experiences openly and honestly with someone who won't judge or use that information against them." I reminded him that I was on his team and had confidence he'd come home and do his thing.

"That's why I love you. I knew the moment I met you that you would seek to understand me and my world. I feel blessed to have such an understanding and thoughtful woman and partner to come home to. I know you're going to help make my transition a lot easier."

"That's all I was trying to do. You can't fault me for wanting to be prepared for your homecoming. I just want to surround you with the love and support you'll need."

"I just want you to be you," Shaka replied, looking into my eyes.

"And I want you to be you. I want you to be free to live, to dream, to build, to be the kind of man and father you were destined to be. I want you to be happy, baby. Genuinely."

44

My thoughts of life with Shaka became more vivid and colorful as his homecoming neared. Sometimes it felt as though he was really there in the room with me. Ten days out, I started my official countdown. I was a ball of nerves. I was excited, but I was also afraid. I heard the women in the discussion forum saying, "You don't *know* him." The reality that our relationship had been defined by his confinement, that longing and loneliness and long poetic letters was all I knew started to settle in. I wondered how we would be once there were no bars between us. Would we still ease in and out of conversation? Would we still hunger for each other? I knew life on the outside would present new challenges but I looked forward to waking up to him in my bed, preparing two plates of food instead of one, hearing him in the next room and remembering I wasn't there alone. I looked forward to facing the unknowns together.

The fact that I was still unemployed scared me more than

anything. I was now behind on my mortgage. I'd bought my house, a two-bedroom brick ranch not much bigger than the one I grew up in, in 2004, and I'd never paid my mortgage late. When I started looking to buy a house, I knew I wanted to be in Detroit. It didn't matter where it was, the east side or the west side, as long as it was a ranch. I felt safer in a one-story house where I could hear unfamiliar sounds or movements, possible signs of a break-in. I'd dreamt of raising a family there and all the daydreams I'd had of me and Shaka together were in that house.

This isn't the life I wanted Shaka to come home to. I'd grown up seeing my mama struggle to make ends meet, mostly on one income. I didn't want that for us.

"It wasn't supposed to be like this," I said to Shaka on one of our last visits, studying my hands, trying to keep from crying.

"I can't imagine how you feel when it comes to the mortgage situation. No one wants to lose a home they've invested so much into, but you have to trust the Creator will make a way for us."

"I do, but what are we going to do in the meantime? I don't even have a car if I did find a job. If I lose the house, where are we going to live?"

"Listen, as long as we're together that's all that matters to me. If we had to live in a shoe until things improved for us, it wouldn't matter as long as we are together."

I sighed, my frustration mixed with relief. He would be home and that meant I wouldn't have to do this alone anymore.

The buildings, the trees, the cars were all a blur. My mind was already in tomorrow as I drove down Eight Mile Road to Mound Correctional Facility. *Just one more day.*

This would be the last time I'd have to endure full body searches, kissing under the watchful eyes of prison guards, eating processed vending machine food. No more waiting on letters. No more 15-minute phone calls. No more sleeping alone.

I pulled into the gated driveway and handed the guard my driver's license. He eyed my picture and then looked up at me.

"Who you here to visit?" he snapped.

"White #219***," I responded. I knew the drill.

I parked the car, a ten-year-old green Honda Civic I'd borrowed from my sister-in-law, and stepped out into the hot Detroit sun. Inside the building, I took in everything around me for the last time—the dull paint on the walls, the tiny green lockers, the clock above the front desk, the speckled tile on the floor—and thought, *We did it.*

I signed in and found the nearest chair. I sat there for what seemed like forever lost in thought, waiting on them to call Shaka's name.

It was his birthday, and it would be the first time we'd ever spent it together. When we learned Shaka would be released on June 22, the day after his thirty-eighth birthday, we knew it wasn't just a coincidence. He'd be starting a new life, a rebirth. Shaka had his whole life ahead of him now, and we'd be building that life together.

"White," the officer barked, jarring me back to reality. I walked through the Plexiglas door, the nervousness I'd had on my first visit long gone. I was a pro now. I raised my arms without her saying a word. The officer rushed her hands across my body. I was one in a long line of bodies she'd have to search that day.

Once I was cleared, I stood at the second Plexiglas door waiting for my turn to enter the visiting room. I could see Shaka through the thick glass panes. He was already seated and waiting. The officer processed two more visitors and then motioned the control center to open the door.

When I entered the visiting room, Shaka's face lit up. I loved it when he smiled, something he rarely did. We hugged, kissed, and then settled into our seats.

"Happy birthday, baby," I said, half singing.

"Thank you, gorgeous."

"Well, this is it. You ready?" I joked.

"Hell yeah! It's about to go down."

We planned our week. Dinner with family. Time with his children, Jay and Lakeisha. Reconnecting with friends. Books.

Of course, books. Shaka couldn't wait to get to work. We'd

only been able to sell a couple hundred copies of *Crack*, mostly through friends and family. Now he'd be able to build the business he'd dreamed of.

That week, Detroit was hosting the U.S. Social Forum and Shaka was invited to participate in a panel and book signing for returning citizens. This would be his first book signing, and a rare opportunity to connect with organizers from all over the world.

"The panel's going to be on Thursday at Wayne County Community College and then the book signing will be on Friday at this riverfront park near the Renaissance Center."

"Cool, I'm going to see if some of my family can make it."

"That would be nice. They'll be able to see you in your element."

"Yeah, I can't wait for them to see me do my thang. I don't think they'll really see the vision until I'm out there." He looked off into the distance, and then continued, "I talked to D. Him and his girl broke up." D had maxed out on his sentence and had been home a year.

"Oh no, I hate to hear that. They been together for a while."

"Yeah, she walked them last two years down with him. But shit wasn't adding up for him once he got home and that took a toll on their relationship. They tried, though, I'll give 'em that. But he had some trust issues, and you know she was a trip."

That would never be us, we said.

We talked for hours as the sun started to set through the small barred windows. When the officer announced, "Visiting hours are now over," we looked at each other and smiled. In just a few hours, we'd be in each other's arms, for good, and this time nothing could keep us apart.

46

The next morning, I climbed out of bed excited to start my day. I'd pictured the day hundreds of times. The drive to pick him up. The nerves. The moment I saw him, free and smiling. The release.

The second my feet touched the floor, a list of to-dos popped up in my head. Wash the dishes. Make the bed. Take a shower. Shave my legs. I made sure everything was in its place. His toothbrush and deodorant, his underwear, his socks. I grabbed the Blackberry I'd bought him and put it in my purse with a short stack of the business cards I'd gotten printed for him. Once I was satisfied I hadn't forgotten anything, I got dressed.

When I slipped on my dress, a short flirty one with ruffles on the sleeves, the butterflies came. I was minutes away from my happily-ever-after.

Around 11am, I headed out to pick up Jay, Shaka's son. Jay was usually quiet and laid back but he walked to the car smiling so big I could see every crease in his thin brown face. He was eighteen now and taller than Shaka, but in his eyes I saw the little boy who missed his father. Jay's mother was three months pregnant with him when Shaka went to prison. He'd only known his father through letters and phone calls and visits. Shaka's homecoming would be a new beginning for him too.

Halfway to the parole office, I got a call from Shaka's parole agent. Shaka was done with whatever paperwork he had to sign and was ready to be picked up. My heart quickened. Shaka had told me I'd be picking him up from the parole office, not the prison like I'd imagined in all my daydreams about his homecoming. He didn't know what time the prison van would drop him off at the parole office or how long it would take him to see his parole officer, so I'd been waiting for that call all morning.

My underarms collected sweat as I inched closer to the building, barely driving the speed limit down Greenfield Road. It felt as if the car was on autopilot, or someone else was driving. I had already fast forwarded in my mind to the next morning, waking up next to Shaka, smelling his sweaty skin after a long night of lovemaking.

When I pulled into the parking lot, Shaka was already outside. He was wearing the outfit I'd bought and left for him at the front desk after one of our last visits. Gray jean shorts, a white Polo shirt, and silver and white Air Force Ones. I had only seen him in his state blues and the handful of shirts and jeans he was allowed to wear on visits. Pretty much every guy who came out on a visit had on the same outfit—a plaid button-up shirt, Wrangler-looking blue jeans, and black state-issued shoes. They all ordered from the same prison-approved clothing catalogue. Now Shaka looked like a regular brother from the hood.

The building was nondescript. There were no signs that read Michigan Department of Corrections or Parole Office, only the faint letters from the CVS sign that used to mark the entrance. I stopped the car right in front of Shaka, who was standing in the middle of the parking lot talking to a brother, jumped out, and ran into his arms.

"Babyyyy!" I screamed, elongating the *e* sound for as long as my lungs would allow.

I wrapped my arms around Shaka's neck. He lifted me up as our bodies collided, our lips finding the familiarity of home. "Oops," I said as the wind caught my dress, exposing me to passersby. We laughed.

Shaka put me back down, then turned and hugged Jay, their first embrace in two years.

"What's up, pops?"

"What's good? You done got taller. And what's that on your face?"

Jay laughed, rubbing the hair on his chin.

"You got some books on you?" Shaka asked, his face turning serious.

I smiled. "Yeah, I got some in the trunk."

He grabbed a copy of *Crack* from the box of books I had in the trunk and handed it to the brother he was talking to when I pulled up.

"Baby, you got a pen? I want to sign this brother's book. This about to be a classic."

He hadn't been free a full hour and he had already made a sale.

I kept looking over at Shaka as we drove away from the parole office. There was something different about him. It wasn't the new clothes, or the new gray in his beard. His eyes were brighter. His smile came easy and often, the weight of his captivity now gone. I couldn't wait to get him all to myself but I knew his family was waiting to see him.

47

We kicked it with Shaka's family for about an hour before we headed home. When I rolled into the driveway, I looked over at Shaka, taking it all in, and I smiled. He turned his face toward mine and kissed me.

"We're home," I sang as our lips parted.

He wasted no time getting out of the car. He stood in the driveway for a good minute looking at the house. "It looks just like the pictures."

I remembered the picture of the house I'd sent him with a photo of us pasted on it to look like we were standing in the front yard. "Let's go inside. I can't wait to give you a tour." We walked, hand in hand, around to the back door. I gave him the keys. "Welcome home, baby."

He tossed the keys around in his hand, feeling the weight of the metal. "Thank you, gorgeous."

I waited anxiously as he opened the door. When he stepped inside, I could see his eyes traveling around the room, recording every detail. We started in the kitchen and I led him from one room to the other. When we got to what was now *our* bedroom, he stood in the doorway.

"Is that my side?" he said, pointing to the right side of the bed, the side closest to the door. I had stopped sleeping on the right side of the bed—his side—a year earlier trying to use the law of attraction to manifest his freedom.

"Yes, and you can put your stuff in that nightstand. That's just for you."

We stare at each other for a full minute, maybe more, and then we kiss, our tongues remembering. He wraps his arms around me and we stand in the middle of the bedroom holding each other. I feel the beat of his heart against my chest and I close my eyes to listen. I lean into his body a little more. His hands explore my curves, his fingers just barely touching my skin. He enjoys seeing my body react to his touch. "I love you," he whispers. Those words feel heavier now. He lifts my dress, pulls it over my head, and steps back to admire my body. "You're perfect." I blush and reach for his shorts. I undo the button, then the zipper, eager to feel him. His shorts fall to the ground as he pulls his shirt over his head. We kiss and kiss and then fall onto the bed. He climbs on top of me and I wrap my legs around his waist as he enters me. We ease into lovemaking like old lovers reunited.

Almost immediately, I felt discomfort, and then pain. Each time Shaka thrust into me, it hurt. Each time, I held my breath and braced myself for the pain. I laid there for what seemed like forever, hoping the pain would go away, or he'd come so it would be over.

Finally, he stopped.

"What's wrong, gorgeous?" he asked with concern in his voice.

"It hurts," I whispered. Tears started to well up in my eyes.

I hadn't had sex in four years. What could be wrong?

I got up from the bed and went to the bathroom to clean myself up. I didn't want to talk but I knew we needed to discuss what had just happened.

"What do you think it is?" Shaka said from the bedroom.

"I don't know. Maybe it's the fibroids." About a year before Shaka and I started corresponding, I learned I had six small uterine fibroids.

"Is this the first time it's hurt like this?" he asked, joining me in the bathroom.

I nodded. I couldn't bring myself to look at him. I felt like a tease. I'd talked so much shit about our first time. My embarrassment quietly turned into fear. *What do we do now? What if I can't fix this?*

We tried again, and again, but each time it hurt. *This is some bullshit*, I thought. I wanted our first time together to be perfect. We'd spent four years fantasizing about that moment, writing the most erotic letters to each other. It was still beautiful, just painful, and certainly not what we imagined. In that moment, all that mattered was he was there, with me. He was home. He was free.

The next morning, I waited for Shaka to rise from a good sleep. I'd been up with the sun. I laid there watching him rest, his face pressed into the pillow, his chest rising and falling. I wondered what he was dreaming about, if free dreams were different from caged dreams. I thought about how just a week earlier he was sleeping in a 5' × 9' cell on a paper-thin mattress with an itchy wool blanket. I wanted to touch him, to run my fingers across his muscled frame or wipe the sweat from his brow, but I was afraid of waking him, of startling him.

"Good morning," I whispered when his eyes finally opened an hour later.

"Good morning, gorgeous."

"You sleep well?"

"Like a baby."

"Good. You hungry?"

We had talked about his first breakfast on one of our last visits and I'd gone grocery shopping to get all the ingredients. French toast, turkey bacon, and orange juice. Shaka sat at the kitchen table while I cooked and we talked about our plans for the day. When I set his plate in front of him, his eyes wide with wonder, I smiled inside. I'd dreamed of catering to him. I'd never seen my mama fix my daddy's plate, or cater to him in any other way, but I'd seen enough women in my family do it and I was happy to finally be able to do it for my man.

48

Shaka sat in between my legs as I oiled his scalp. His hair was just washed and gave way to my fingers as I parted it. We talked as I twisted his untamed mane, now peppered with gray, pulling apart the locs that had started growing together. He leaned into me, finding comfort in the warmth of my thighs.

"How does it feel being home?" I asked. "Has it sunk in yet?"

"It still feels surreal."

"Has it been what you expected so far?"

"For the most part. It's been cool to hang out with my pops and the fam. I know it's going to take some time to rebuild those relationships. My pops is the only one who really knows me. I'm not the same person I was nineteen years ago. They know me as Jay or Pumpkin, not Shaka."

"Yeah, I hear them calling you Pumpkin. It might take a minute for them to get used to calling you Shaka."

"I'm not tripping."

"I love it when they call you Pumpkin though."

"I know you do," he laughed.

We eased in and out of conversation like we always did. We sat there like that for more than an hour, talking, and then I got up.

"Where you going?"

"The kitchen." I asked him if he wanted anything.

"Nah, I'm good."

Thirty minutes later, when I got up from the couch again to go to the bathroom, he asked, "Where you going?"

He did this every time I moved. After two weeks, I wanted to scream. I didn't. I'd answer him, exasperated. I wasn't used to answering so many questions about my movements. I was used to living alone. I was used to being . . . free.

I'd taken my freedom for granted, and underestimated how much prison had robbed Shaka of his.

Shaka told me he didn't want me to hold his hand when he came home, so I didn't. I encouraged him to explore and challenged him to think instead of giving him an immediate answer. But after a couple weeks, he started saying, "Just tell me."

He was eager to learn everything he could about social media. Once he got the hang of it, he started writing short pieces and sharing them on Facebook. He enjoyed the responses to his writing and eventually started writing longer essays. Instead of long poetic letters, he would post romantic messages on my timeline. "Have I told you today how much I love your smile and the sound of your laughter? It is always fun when we just lie in the bed laughing, joking, and kicking it."

Soon he started introducing me to Facebook features I didn't know about.

Driving was a different animal. Shaka had only walked, or rode in the back of a prison van, for nineteen years. He was nervous about getting behind the wheel. I drove for the first few weeks, and when he was ready, he took the Honda I was still driving around the block a couple times. It didn't take him long to get comfortable on the road, but he had to relearn the city. He'd call me when he needed directions.

"Do I make a right or a left when I get to Warren?"

"A right."

A minute later, still on the phone, he'd ask again. "Do I make a right or left?"

"A right."

Then again, when it was time to make the turn, "Did you say a right?"

"Shaka, I just told you a right. Were you listening?" I tried my best to be patient, not to show my frustration, but eventually all the questions started annoying me and my Black-girl attitude edged its way into our conversations.

"You're too impatient," he told me.

Soon the arguments came. I was tired of the questions. He was tired of my short answers. "This is just part of my personality," I kept telling him. "This is how every Black woman I know talks." But Shaka didn't want to hear any of that. He had just come from an environment where guys with smart mouths got stabbed or beaten. There is no sorry in prison. Violence is the only response that gets respect.

Shaka had earned a reputation in prison as someone who

could hold his own and his natural leadership qualities made him stand apart. "You have to understand, no one ever talked smart to me. Ever. That was my life for nineteen years. When I needed something done, no one questioned me or backtalked. They did what was asked. That's the law of the jungle in there."

"I get it. But do you understand you're asking me to change the way I've talked my entire life? That's not easy."

"I'm just asking you to change the way you talk to *me*," he laughed, breaking the tension. "But for real, when you talk to me like that, it reminds me of the way my mother used to talk to me," he continued, his face now serious.

I knew how his mother had physically and verbally abused him. It hurt to hear him say that. "Wow, is it that bad? I'll try to be more conscious of my words." I certainly didn't want to be like his mama, or mine.

The more we argued, however, the harder it grew to reel my Black-girl attitude in, and before long, our communication broke down completely.

49

appy birthday, gorgeous," Shaka whispered, turning onto his side. I had been up for an hour already, lying in the bed thinking. It felt like time was flying. I remembered counting down the days to his homecoming and there we were, a month later, like it had always been that way.

"What do you want to do today?"

"I'm open, but I definitely want to do brunch at Inn Season."

"That's that vegetarian spot, right?"

I smiled.

"No turkey bacon?" he joked.

"Nope, not today."

"I'm good. Anything for you, baby."

After brunch we went down to the riverfront, one of my favorite destinations in Detroit. We found a quiet spot along the river's edge and sat down on two big rocks sitting shaded by a small tree. We dreamed like we always did, but we also reminisced.

"Shaka," I began. "Do you have any regrets?"

Shaka looked into the distance, and then turned back to me. "My only regret is that I didn't find you sooner. Us connecting while I was in there was the best thing. It allowed me room to grow in the ways I needed in order to be the husband you need. Some of the conflicts we had we needed to experience in order to be the power couple we are destined to become."

"While it was hard in every way imaginable, I agree. I wouldn't change a thing. We have grown together as a couple in ways that were only possible through the things we've experienced."

"And we're still growing, individually and together. I know things have been kind of rough, but our love is strong."

We sat there into the late afternoon and evening, talking, watching the waves lap against the shore.

The Detroit River became our sanctuary. Some nights we'd drive downtown and walk along the riverfront, laughing and talking and people-watching the way we did on visits. Sometimes, when we weren't getting along, I'd go by myself, often with my journal, and meditate.

I watched from the kitchen window as Shaka stood in the backyard puffing on a Black & Mild. He'd started smoking the long, thin cigars on his first day home. I hated smoking, and he knew it. He told me to give him two weeks and he'd stop. I wanted him to enjoy his freedom, so I didn't trip. But two weeks came and went, and he was still smoking.

"I thought you said you were going to quit," I said when he came into the house.

Shaka glared at me. "I got this."

Every time he lit up a cigar, I took a deep breath and pretended not to care. I did the same when he drank. Everyone joked about how much alcohol Shaka could drink without getting drunk. After watching my daddy drink himself to death, I wasn't amused.

I was fourteen when I had my first drink, Boone's Farm. We were on a class field trip and someone on the bus started passing around the cheap wine. I drank just enough to feel a buzz. I liked the way I felt. I could be someone I wasn't—funny, charismatic, free. But that feeling also terrified me. I remembered my daddy, so drunk some days he could barely walk. I ended up not drinking again until I was in college, and even then, even now, I don't drink more than two drinks.

Shaka's drinking triggered memories of the life I once tried to hide. Empty liquor bottles in the trash. Drunken sleep. Late nights up hoping he made it home safely. But he didn't see a problem. "I got this," he told me again.

Most nights, Shaka hung out with his family or friends, leaving me home alone. Initially, we went together to backyard barbeques or pop-up get-togethers but I got tired of sitting around somebody's basement or backyard watching him drink.

I carried the burden of making Shaka's freedom all that he wanted it to be. I wasn't trying to make it harder. I didn't nag him about the hanging out. I didn't nag him about the drinking, or the smoking. I didn't want to be *that* girlfriend, so I kept my thoughts to myself.

50

Shaka couldn't wait to start building a buzz for *Crack*, and less than two months after he came home, we did a city-wide book tour. We chose four venues across the city and I designed a flyer. We spread the word mostly via social media and word-of-mouth from our family and friends.

The tour gave Shaka a jolt of energy. He was in his element. Talking to people. Signing books. Guys he knew from prison came out to support, and guys who were still locked up sent family. Old friends from the hood even stopped by.

"This is just the beginning," Shaka told me on the second day. "We got to do a national tour. Hit New York, and maybe Chicago and Atlanta. New York is still popping when it comes to street lit."

"Yeah, maybe we can do the Harlem Book Fair next year."

"That's in July, right?"

I nodded.

"I want to do something before then, but we'll see."

After the book tour, Shaka sold *Crack* out of the trunk of the Honda, crisscrossing the city to meet up with anyone who said they wanted a book. He'd come home at the end of the day with stories about who he'd met and where he'd been.

By the end of the summer, Shaka landed a freelance gig working for a local newspaper. He started out writing album reviews and then they asked him to write features for the Arts and Culture section. Once again, he was in his element. Talking to people. Writing stories.

One night he came home, waking me up from a good sleep, frustrated with the pace of book sales. The pressure to succeed had begun to take its toll. The books were moving but not as fast as he'd hoped, and money was tight.

"I can't do this anymore, Eb. I'm tired of spinning my wheels and getting nowhere. This book shit ain't adding up." There was an urgency in his voice.

"Baby, I know it's been hard but it's going to be okay. *We're* going to be okay."

"I'm tired of you telling me that. That shit ain't paying the bills. I can't have you out here doing this alone."

I continued listening without trying to make him feel better. I knew nothing else I said would change how he felt.

"I'm thinking about hollering at one of my guys," he said after a long pause.

I knew what that meant. I was half-sleep, but I woke up when I heard those words. Lots of guys succumb to the pressure of trying to rebuild a life and find legitimate work. But I knew Shaka was stronger than that. His dreams were too big. I lifted the bass in my voice, and with my fiercest tired-

Black-woman face, I said, "That's not what I signed up for. If you go back to the streets, I'm done."

Even though things had been slower than he expected, Shaka had only been home a few months. I hadn't lost faith in him. I needed him not to lose faith either.

We talked into the wee hours of the morning and I reiterated in no uncertain terms that I would not sit around and watch him ruin his life.

51

Shaka held my hand as I listened to my gynecologist tell me that the pain I was experiencing during sex was likely caused by the fibroids. She suspected they'd grown.

"There are some surgical options and some nonsurgical options. We can do a myomectomy, which would remove the fibroids and keep the uterus intact, or embolization, which would cut off the blood supply to the fibroids. Do you plan to have children?"

"Yes." I looked at Shaka. We had talked about starting a family but decided to wait until he got on his feet.

"Wonderful. Well the embolization is less intrusive. It will shrink the fibroids, but they may grow back."

"Will they grow back with the myomectomy?"

"Yes, there's a small chance."

I did not like my options. I decided to try to eliminate the fibroids naturally. I went online and researched natural remedies for shrinking fibroids. Like with the acne, my diet was an important element. I eliminated dairy and cut back on carbs and sweets, and then had a series of colonics once a month for three months to remove any toxins in my body that might have been causing the fibroids to grow.

Shaka and I continued to have sex. Lots of it. We experimented with positions and found some that worked. Eventually, after the third colonic, I noticed a difference. Sex was less painful.

Then one night, getting ready for bed, Shaka told me he wanted to talk to me about something. "I've been having these desires," he started. He wanted to be with other women. His words hung there in the air, heavy.

I felt stupid. Foolish to believe I was the only woman he would need. He'd told me, over and over again, "I don't want any other woman. Meaningless sex doesn't appeal to me. I know what a blessing you are, and I would be a fool to squander it for a tryst with some empty woman who couldn't begin to comprehend the kind of man I am. You and I are worth so much more."

"You promised me you were different," I cried.

"I thought you'd understand," Shaka replied. "If anybody knows what I've been through, you do."

I wasn't sure what he wanted me to say or how he expected me to respond, but I broke down in tears, angry, confused, and heartbroken.

"Understand what? You said you were different."

He grew defensive. "Other guys would have kept their desires to themselves and just cheated." I was lucky, he said.

"What now?"

"I don't know," he admitted. He was still grappling with it himself, he said. "None of this changes how I feel about you."

I tucked Shaka's words away in the back of my mind. I did not know what to do with them. We had made a promise to be together forever. I hadn't expected this.

For weeks I wrestled with whether to stay and fight for our relationship or let him go so he could truly be free. I didn't want to be like my mama, holding on when I should let go. But letting go would prove all the naysayers right.

52

"Did you fuck her?" I screamed into the phone as soon as Shaka answered. I'd looked through his email and found a message from a woman he had worked with on a story for the paper. A woman I had befriended. She said she loved how soft his lips were. Do you think Ebony suspects anything?

"What are you talking about?" he responded.

"You know what I'm talking about! Did you fuck her?"

"Look, I'm at work. We'll talk about this when I get home," he said calmly, trying to rush me off the phone.

"No, we gone talk about this right now!" I insisted, tears streaming down my face, my cheeks red with anger, my body filled with the same rage I imagine my mama felt the night she screamed for Daddy's girlfriend to come out of the closet and show herself.

"Look, Ebony, I'm at work. I can't talk about this right now."

I knew the answer to my question. "I hate you! I hate you! How could you?"

I pictured Shaka doing things to this other woman that he had done to me. I couldn't get those images out of my mind.

My eyes were swollen red and my mouth dry from doing nothing but crying by the time Shaka got home that night. We stood in the kitchen as far apart from each other as possible, him leaning against the stove, his eyes fixed on me, cold and indifferent to my questions. I wanted him to say, "Baby, I'm sorry. Baby, please forgive me." Instead he offered four simple words. "What did you expect?"

I stood there in disbelief. His tone was one of indignation, as if I had done something wrong; as if I had been crazy for wanting him to only make love to me.

Shaka's question was absent any empathy for my pain. In his mind, he'd been in prison since he was a teenager. What *did* I expect?

I never expected Shaka to be perfect, but I did expect him to be the man he told me he was—principled, fiercely loyal, and honest. I questioned everything he had ever said to me. "I'd never hurt you," he reassured me, letter after letter, year after year. "Nothing or no one will ever come between us." Promises made from the safety of prison.

I thought about our letters, about all the years I'd waited for him to be released. Was our love a lie?

I'd said cheating was one of my deal breakers. I'd said I wouldn't be my mama and stay with a man who cheated on me. But sitting there with just six months of freedom, the answers weren't so cut and dried.

Several days later, the woman he had fucked sent me a message on Facebook, blaming Shaka for everything. All the emotions I had the day I found out came rushing back. I hit Shaka in the arm over and over. Once I calmed down, I read the message to him. "He came on to me. One night we met up for drinks and he kissed me. It just spiraled from there. I didn't mean for any of this to happen."

"I'm sorry," Shaka said finally. I'd been waiting for an apology, an acknowledgment of my pain. He reached to kiss me. I didn't turn away.

I never uttered a word to anyone about the other woman. Not Kim. Not Malik. And certainly not my mama. I was good at keeping secrets.

Back when Shaka's homecoming was too far away to get too excited, I had one idea about freedom. I just wanted him home. Everything else would work itself out. But freedom was not what either of us expected.

5 3

Soon after we rung in the New Year, I learned the house was officially in foreclosure. I'd gotten a part-time job, but what I earned and what Shaka brought home from writing freelance and selling books wasn't enough to cover the mortgage and our other expenses. I was now months behind on my mortgage. The country was starting to climb out of the Great Recession, but Michigan was one of the states hardest hit. I'd spent more than a year looking for a job, but I was either overqualified or underqualified for the limited jobs available. I applied for a government-sponsored mortgage modification program in an attempt to save my home, but after months of negotiation, my bank only lowered my mortgage payment by $100. That wasn't enough.

One night I came home from my part-time job, tired and ready to collapse into the bed, and found a small gold box and a letter sitting on my pillow. Inside the box was a pair of heart-shaped diamond studs. A smile broke through. The tension in my shoulders fell away. I forgot, temporarily, about the pain of betrayal. I opened the letter eager to see what beautiful words awaited me.

"Knowing that I hurt the woman I love more than anyone has been the hardest thing for me to deal with. I know I have come across as being insensitive and uncaring and I apologize wholeheartedly because I truly love you. But know that it has never been my intent to hurt you. I just didn't know how to make things right. To not have you in my life would destroy my heart. I don't want to break up, but some days I just want to break free from all the drama that we created. I know all of this is a necessary part of our growth as a couple, and we just have to ride out the storm when it comes. They say diamonds are forever so take this small gift as a token of how long I plan to love you, be there for you, and cherish you. I love you from the depths of my soul."

This is the man I know. I missed Shaka's notes and letters. His gesture warmed my heart. We're gonna be all right, I thought to myself as I folded his letter and tucked it away in my nightstand.

We started talking about getting a fresh start. We didn't have to move right away but Shaka was eager to start our new chapter.

"I don't like the idea of this foreclosure looming over our heads. We need some stability. I've been home seven months and I don't feel settled. I need to be able to focus."

"I hear you. I'm not sure how long we'll be able to stay here, and I don't want to come home to a letter that says we got thirty days to move. I'll see what I can find online."

We found a two-bedroom townhouse in Woodbridge, a De-troit neighborhood close to Wayne State University and down-town. We were nervous about our application—Shaka had to provide the details of his crime. Many apartment communities don't rent to individuals with a felony conviction, but after two days of waiting we found out we'd been approved.

Packing was bittersweet. I was sad to leave my first house, the home I thought I'd raise my babies in, but I was happy not to have the responsibility. Every year there was something. The first year, my property taxes more than doubled. The following year, my homeowner's insurance went up, and then the hot water heater went out. I'd been stressed trying to make ends meet and now I could breathe.

We were still unpacking when I noticed my period was late. It arrived every month like clockwork on the twenty-eighth day.

"I think I'm pregnant," I told Shaka.

He smiled. "I think you are, too. Something seems different about you."

"Should I go get a pregnancy test, or just wait until tomor-row? My annual exam is in the morning."

"Just wait. But I know you're pregnant. I can feel it."

Two days later, my gynecologist called me with the news. "You're pregnant," she said, her voice full of excitement. In-stantly, I could feel something in the deepest part of me growing.

We had not planned to start a family that soon, but we hadn't taken precautions not to. I knew we weren't ready, but I didn't care. I had never been pregnant, and at thirty-five I knew my chances of getting pregnant were shrinking each year we waited. I welcomed the idea of a baby, the reality of a baby, with joy not fear, anticipation not dread.

I'd just gotten a full-time job after being unemployed for over a year and I was scheduled to start the next day. My excitement was mixed with apprehension. How and when would I tell my new boss? Shaka and I agreed I should wait until I made it through my first trimester. In the meantime, we told our closest family and friends. I couldn't read Mama's response. She'd warmed up to Shaka, but I think somewhere in the back of her mind, she didn't want us to work out. I ignored what seemed to be disappointment and went on and on about how excited I was. This is *my* moment, I told myself.

There was another life growing inside me and I took this responsibility seriously. I found vegan prenatal vitamins and became even more conscious of my diet. I turned on jazz while I drove or listened to the quiet, calming sounds of meditation music. Every day, I touched my belly and wondered at the life we'd created. For the first time in a long time, I was happy.

I wanted to give my baby the loving two-parent household I never had. Building a strong family was something Shaka and I talked about all the time, not just because of our broken childhoods, but because we knew healthy Black families were needed to heal the Black community. We wanted to be a model of Black family life. We wanted to continue the legacy of our ancestors and work together with our children for the advancement of our people. And we were about to have that chance.

was excited about motherhood, especially to share the experience with Shaka. I knew he would be a great father. He wasn't able to be the kind of father he wanted to be to Jay and Lakeisha. This time he'd be there to wipe away tears and see first steps. He'd be able to teach and guide and nurture.

But Shaka's enthusiasm was coupled with anxiety. He wasn't working the freelance gig anymore and didn't have a reliable source of income. I could support our growing family on my new salary, but Shaka wasn't having it.

"Eb, I can't let you do this alone," he insisted. "I've got to do my part. That's what fathers do."

I tried to convince him that we'd be okay. "I know, baby, but I don't want you to stress. I got this."

"I got this" is what I always said, but my words did not comfort Shaka. In fact, they angered him. His sense of pride, his manhood wouldn't allow him to let me be the primary breadwinner, and my efforts to ease his stress only made him resent me. Maybe it was the euphoria of new motherhood, but I did not have the fears Shaka had.

He started feeling more and more stressed as my belly grew. I never pressured him about getting a job, but he felt the weight of his unemployment mounting the closer we got to the baby's December due date. He applied for jobs that seemed perfect for him—youth counselor, nonprofit program manager—but kept getting turned down. He had no work experience. No degree. I tried gussying up his resume, playing up his experience in prison mentoring and tutoring younger inmates. Finally, he was invited for an interview.

"I killed it, Eb. They seemed really impressed with my ideas."

"That's awesome. When did they say they'd get back to you?"

"Sometime next week . . . I think I got it." His eyes were bright again.

When he got the call that they'd chosen someone else, Shaka took it hard. He moped around the house for weeks. Then finally, he decided to go back to school. In September, he enrolled in a one-year design program where he studied graphic design, photography, and video editing. He came home every week excited about all the new things he was learning.

We continued to prepare for the baby's arrival and settled on a name—Sekou Akili. Sekou means "fighter" and Akili means "bright, intelligent." The perfect name for our little warrior prince.

I loved feeling Sekou move around in my belly. It was an amazing experience.

It was a Wednesday, July 31, when I felt Sekou move

around for the first time. I was lying down, getting ready to fall asleep, and I felt a light tap in my belly. Other moms told me it would feel like butterflies fluttering around in my stomach, or popcorn popping, but I didn't feel butterflies or popcorn—the feeling was actually indescribable—but after that night, I could feel Sekou move all the time.

"Baby, he's moving. Come here, quickly," I whispered to Shaka one day. He hadn't felt Sekou move. Every time I felt him stirring, either Shaka wasn't with me or by the time he put his hand on my belly, Sekou had stopped. Shaka smiled as he reached for my baby bump. I looked at him and gently laid my hand on top of his. We didn't say a word for fear that we would startle Sekou and he'd stop moving. We stared at each other as we felt our baby boy twisting and turning inside my womb. "Hey, little man," Shaka whispered, grinning from ear to ear.

55

was about twenty-five when I started feeling my biological clock ticking. I thought I'd be swept off my feet and have a couple babies before I turned thirty, but by the time I met Shaka, I was thirty with no babies. The decision I had made to wait for him meant delaying the dream of motherhood further.

Of all the things I dreamed about, what was most important was that my children be raised in a loving home where they could grow into healthy, conscious, productive men and women who were committed to changing the conditions in our community. I didn't care about being married. I didn't care about the "right time." Unlike my mama. She'd pleaded with me, "Just finish high school before you start having babies." Then she pleaded, "Just finish college." And then, "Just finish grad school." It was never the right time. I knew why she wanted me to wait to have children. Children would make life harder, and she wanted more for me than she'd had.

I savored every moment of my pregnancy. I never had

morning sickness or many of the other symptoms moms-to-be often experience. Even with Shaka and me constantly arguing, I stayed in a peaceful place. I knew everything I consumed, from unhealthy food to unhealthy thoughts, Sekou was consuming too. Stress can be felt by babies in utero so whenever I felt anxious or overwhelmed, I meditated or went down by the Detroit River and wrote in my journal.

But I struggled to find peace when we got the results of my prenatal genetic tests. I was thirty-five years old when Sekou was conceived and the doctors recommended we do genetic testing.

"There's an eighty percent chance your baby will have Downs Syndrome," the doctor told us. "We'd like to do an amniocentesis. We would take a small sample of the amniotic fluid and run some additional tests that would allow us to examine the fetal DNA closer."

My heart sank. Shaka and I went home and cried like we cried when he got flopped the second time. We discussed our options. We agreed that we didn't want any further testing. I was already in love. It didn't matter what the tests said.

Every day I poured love into Sekou, reading positive affirmations and listening to music that made me smile. Michael Jackson. Fela Kuti. Stevie Wonder. Shaka and I read to him almost every night, me reading one of the many children's books I had collected and Shaka reading from his library of books on African philosophy and history. Reading to Sekou made us feel closer to him, and each other.

We never talked about the test results again, not to each other or anyone else. I continued to enjoy my pregnancy, choosing to push fear of the unknown aside.

56

The contractions came every 30 seconds, hard and fast. It seemed as soon as one contraction subsided, the next one started, more intense than the last. I had no breaks in between to catch my breath or otherwise brace myself for the next unforgiving wave. "I can't do it! I can't take this anymore," I·cried. "I want an epidural." I had planned to have a natural birth. No drugs. No surgery. But I was beginning to have second thoughts. After hours of intense labor, an epidural started to sound like a good idea.

"Yes you can, baby. You can do it," Shaka encouraged me. "Remember how much you wanted to have a natural birth. I don't want you to look back and have any regrets. You can do it. I know you can."

Hours earlier, we were sitting in the doctor's office for our weekly visit. I was 41 weeks and there were no signs of labor— Sekou was chillin. "You need to be induced," my doctor announced, and an hour later I was lying in a hospital bed with a heart monitor attached to my belly.

Shaka kept me grounded as the contractions grew and the glow I'd worn for my entire pregnancy disappeared. He cheered me on through those last few hours of the worst pain ever, then stood by my side as I pushed Sekou out just after midnight. I laid there afterward, exhausted and numb, while he cut the umbilical cord. Once I caught my breath and my body stopped shaking from eight hours of intense labor, Shaka handed Sekou to me and we stared together in awe at our healthy baby boy. This was the life we had imagined all those days dreaming together in the visiting room.

That night as I watched Sekou sleep, I prayed. I prayed that the world would greet him with love, that they would see his brilliance, his light, his potential. That they would not try to derail his future before he got to live it. I sat with the reality that we would be raising a Black boy in a world that is threatened by Black male presence. A world that despises Black joy. Before he's barely a man, we'll have to teach him the reality of being Black and male in America. I wanted to keep him safe from the world, but I also wanted him to explore it. I wondered how I would raise a free Black boy, a boy who was not afraid to shine his light, to be or do whatever he wanted. I prayed for wisdom, for courage. I prayed for grace.

57

Shaka and I didn't sleep that first night in the hospital. Too much adrenaline. We took turns holding Sekou all night and then sleepiness arrived. In between naps, I tried to nurse but struggled getting Sekou to latch on. I was frustrated that I wasn't getting it "right." I blamed myself. That afternoon, the nurse asked if Sekou had peed yet. He hadn't. By the evening, he still hadn't latched on. And he still hadn't peed. The doctors and nurses suggested we give Sekou formula to encourage his first pee.

I refused their advice. I fought tooth and nail with the nurses for a whole day, then eventually caved in at the end of day two and gave Sekou a few ounces of formula. I continued trying to get him to latch on but by then I was flustered and stressed, which didn't help the latching process.

Hours after I'd given Sekou the formula, he still hadn't peed. The nurses insisted I give him more ounces. Then the doctors stepped in.

"We'd like to run some tests to see how his kidneys are functioning. We'll have to give him an IV and run a dye through his body, so we can see how everything's working," one doctor explained.

We refused.

After the doctors and nurses all left, I held Sekou and told him I loved him. I whispered the words in his tiny brown ear, over and over again, as I held him close, bare chest to bare chest. He knew nothing of the doctors who wanted to poke and prod him, or the nurses who were impatient with him, with me. He was taking his time, this warrior child of mine who was un-bothered by the world buzzing around him. This strong-willed boy who decided to come into the world when he was good and ready, one whole week past his due date. I knew he would pee.

Going into day three, I continued trying to nurse Sekou and supplemented with formula. Ultimately, the doctors forced our hand and said Sekou couldn't go home until he peed.

I cried and prayed as we walked through the labyrinth of floors and elevators to the hospital's Neonatal Intensive Care Unit. I tried to pull myself together as I handed Sekou's tiny brown body to the nurse. Shaka and I held our breath as the nurse opened his diaper. It was soaking wet. *Thank you*, I whispered over and over, this time tears of joy flowing.

I finally got Sekou to latch on once we were away from the stress of the hospital. He was otherwise healthy and normal. We enjoyed those first few months of parenthood. I was on ma-ternity leave, which gave me precious time to bond with Sekou and enjoy being a new mommy. Shaka happily stepped into his role as daddy, changing diapers, reading books, and entertain-ing Sekou while I made dinner. We made a great team.

After four months, I returned to work part-time and Shaka stayed home with Sekou whenever I had meetings. But by the time I went back to work full-time, Shaka told me to get a babysitter. "I'm not about to be daddy daycare," he said.

Most days, I worked from home and Sekou was with me all day. I juggled his needs in between calls and responding to emails and stayed up half the night nursing every 2 to 3 hours like clockwork. Between work and motherhood, I was exhausted every day. One day, when Sekou was about nine months, I asked Shaka if he would stay home with Sekou one night a week, so I could get some me time.

"Take him to your mother's," he responded, his face closed, staring blankly.

I stared back for a good minute and then walked away.

I desperately needed a break. I needed to breath. I needed to walk away from the dirty diapers, the needing, for just a few hours. But I didn't say this to Shaka. I said nothing. I buried my feelings, not even venting to friends. I didn't want him to think I didn't appreciate the things he *did* do. Nothing in his life seemed to be going well—we were still arguing, his relationship with Jay was strained, the book business wasn't going well, and he couldn't find a job. Sekou was a bright spot amid all the chaos in his life and I couldn't bring myself to take the little joy he had.

58

That winter, the Knight Foundation announced a grant competition for Black men who were doing work in their community. Shaka had been speaking and mentoring across the city and wanted to start his own afterschool mentoring program, one of the dreams he had when he was in prison.

"These young guys are wearing rest in peace shirts in honor of their dead homies. I want to change that narrative. I want them to wanna *live* in peace, not just rest in peace."

"I love it. We can do some shirts."

"Right, that's what I was thinking. You're a dope artist. I know you'll design something hot."

The two of us were at our best when we were working on a project together.

"So what do you want to call it?"

We tossed around a few ideas, and then Shaka said, "I got it. The Live in Peace Digital and Literary Arts Project."

Shaka applied for the grant, and with online votes from family and friends, he won the grant competition. We got started right away fleshing out his idea. We decided to build the program around his story, and using the graphic design and editing skills he'd just learned, he would help the students tell their stories. I designed the curriculum and we published a companion book that included some of Shaka's writing and activities to help the students unpack their childhood pain.

Shaka continued speaking in front of school and church groups, at Stop the Violence rallies, and community forums. The more he shared, the more people wanted to know. I want to finish my memoir, he told me. He'd been grinding trying to sell his novels, but his life story was resonating with people in ways the fictional street tales had not. He'd started writing about his life in the streets and in prison before he came home and was halfway done.

Soon after Sekou's first birthday, we self-published Shaka's memoir, just as we'd done his other books. I edited and laid out the manuscript, designed the cover, and did all the promo. "This book is about to change the game," Shaka bragged.

Before long, the speaking gigs picked up and Shaka was able to do more of what he loved—speaking to youth about the not-so-glamorous side of the streets. A year later he was invited to do a TED Talk at TED's 30th Anniversary Conference in Vancouver, British Columbia. That talk led to more talks and before we knew it Shaka was traveling across the country speaking in front of celebrities and influencers from every major industry. It was his dream come true. I worked behind the scenes, drafting press materials, designing promotional pieces, booking speaking engagements, and writing grant proposals for Shaka's mentoring work.

Things were going really well, but eventually, old tensions arose. We had different ideas of what it meant to be partners in business. Shaka felt like I wasn't doing enough, I felt like I was doing everything I could in between my full-time job and motherhood.

59

We quickly outgrew our two-bedroom townhouse once Sekou was born. With all three of us at home most of the time, the townhouse stayed cluttered and there was nowhere to store anything.

Shaka didn't want to move.

"The rent is only eighty hundred and fifty dollars. If we stay, we can save some money."

"I hear you, but I feel like I'm about to lose my mind. I can't stay here another year." The space seemed to be getting smaller and smaller, and the sounds of ongoing traffic from the nearby expressway and the smell of sewage in the basement had become too much.

I started looking online for houses and apartments to rent, and then enlisted the help of a Realtor, but we couldn't find what we wanted within our budget. We wrestled with whether to buy or continue renting. Neither of us felt ready for the responsibility of owning a house, but Shaka's felony was like a scarlet letter on every rental application we submitted. After the housing manager did the criminal background check, we were politely told our application had been denied.

"What if we don't put your name on the lease?"

"Nah, that's not gonna work. I need to have a key. If you're the only person on the lease, they're only going to give us one key."

"Damn, that's right."

"And I don't want to risk them finding out I'm living there and put us out."

After much discussion, and several denied applications, we decided to buy a house. We looked in Detroit, and then the suburbs. Shaka's travel schedule meant Sekou and I were often at home alone and he said he'd feel better if we were in the burbs. I am a diehard Detroiter and didn't want to leave the city, but I agreed.

Months later, we were still looking. We couldn't find a house we both liked. I preferred the houses with old charm and character and he wanted something modern. One day, tired of looking at houses and getting closer and closer to the end of our lease, Shaka told me, "If we don't find a house this week, we're staying here." I didn't like having that kind of pressure—buying a home is a big purchase—but that week we saw a house we liked in Westland, a Detroit suburb. It was a brand-new home in a new subdivision and we could make it our own. We would have more than enough space and Shaka could have a man cave.

I was excited about the move. I thought Shaka was, too. I knew he'd been frustrated with the process, but he'd gotten what he wanted—a modern home with new finishes and a blank canvas to build the man cave of his dreams. But months after we closed, during one of our arguments, he told me I'd forced him into buying a home. "I didn't want this house," he said. Every time an expense came up, I was reminded, "This was your idea. This is your house."

I thought we were making lemonade out of the lemons we had, but Shaka thought I had been controlling and manipulative. Our relationship was already in trouble and the house did nothing but create another wedge between us.

No matter how much we argued, we never stayed mad for more than a couple hours. Before the end of the day we would be laughing again as if nothing had happened. One day after an argument, Shaka told me he had sent a text, a picture, intended for me to my mama.

"What was it?"

"You don't want to know," he said shaking his head.

"It was *that* bad?"

"Yeah."

"Did you say anything with the pic?"

He nodded, guilt all over his face.

"Oh my God, you gotta call my mama and tell her it was a mistake."

He showed me the picture, a woman bent over with honey dripping from her vagina. "How am I going to explain that?"

"I don't know, but you have to call her," I insisted. Seconds later, my phone rang. It was my mama. My mouth dropped. I stared at Shaka with pleading eyes and whispered, "Fix this."

"Hey, Ma," I said calmly, trying to pretend I didn't know why she was calling, waiting on her to tell me about the text, but she didn't say anything.

I handed the phone to Shaka. "Fix this!" I pleaded again.

The minute he put the phone to his ear, he started laughing hysterically.

I looked, confused, and then realized he'd pranked me with my mama's help. I laughed and laughed until I cried. I thought about the look on my mama's face if she'd actually gotten that text and laughed some more.

It was moments like this that reminded me why I loved Shaka.

60

We argued. We made up. We argued. We made love. And the cycle repeated. We never fixed anything. Making up didn't mean we had resolved the issue. We buried it, we moved on, and then we dug it up again. I was stuck in the same cycle as my parents.

A few months after we moved, on a hot August night, I got a text from Shaka after one of our heated arguments. "I'm ready to move on."

I simply replied, "Okay." I didn't cry or question why. I was exhausted from trying to make things work.

Once we had a chance to talk, we agreed he'd move out and I'd stay in our new home with Sekou. We'd give ourselves a year.

We searched for his new apartment together with the help of Toni, the same Realtor who'd found our house in Westland. After three weeks of searching, Toni found a one-bedroom condo in Detroit that Shaka loved. We discussed how he should handle the felony.

"This is a private owner instead of a management company," Toni explained. "Your chances of getting approved are much better."

"What do you think about attaching my bio to the application?"

"That's a good idea. It won't hurt."

I forwarded Toni a copy of Shaka's media kit and she sent it along with his application. We hoped the owner would focus on his accomplishments and not his crime. After a day or two of waiting, she called with the good news.

That fall, with the help of friends, Shaka moved into his new home. I helped him shop for furniture and linens and hung his artwork. I was excited for him. He had never lived on his own as an adult, one of many experiences he'd missed out on while he was in prison.

Every night at Sekou's bedtime, I'd call Shaka so he could do affirmations, a nightly ritual he had started with Sekou months earlier.

"I am brilliant," Shaka began.

"I am brilliant," repeated Sekou in his little voice.

I am kind, I am strong, I am a warrior, he continued, Sekou repeating each line after him. Then finally, with great enthusiasm, Sekou would say, "I am Sekou!"

This wasn't how we wanted to raise Sekou, in two separate homes, but we knew if our relationship was ever going to work, we needed some space.

61

A separation sounded good, but we never left each other alone. Shaka had moved, but he was in between my place and his.

I became obsessed with who he was seeing and drilled him constantly—how did he meet her, what did she look like, did he like her, how much time did they spend together. I was afraid he'd fall in love with someone else. I regularly checked his phone records, text messages, emails, instant messenger, and then four months into our separation, snooping through Shaka's phone one night, I learned about two women he'd been with while we were still together.

I screamed, I cried, I lashed out in anger.

"This is fucked up. The one person I thought had my back, the one I trusted with my heart didn't give a fuck about me. I know I'm not perfect, but I didn't deserve any of this. I feel like a damned fool. We have been down this road before and I told you then how I felt about this shit. All I asked you to do is be real with me. It's fucked up that a relationship that had so much potential has come to this."

Shaka listened. He apologized. I woke up the next morning to an email that started, "Where did we go wrong?"

"I can't sleep because I can't stop thinking about how much I have fucked you over in the last three and a half years. I can't understand why I have hurt you the way I have. Every day I find myself trying to find the answer to the question WHAT THE FUCK IS WRONG WITH ME? I have failed you and our relationship. I fear that the damage I have caused is beyond repair and that worries me. I don't want to lose you, our friendship, or our family. We have gone through many obstacles and been challenged on every front, but this is different because I am the source of your pain and heartbreak."

I read and reread his words. And then hit reply. "I don't know if the damage is beyond repair, but I know this shit hurts like fucking hell and I'm afraid of being a fool again."

That night, after putting Sekou to bed, I wrapped myself in a blanket, grabbed a corner of the couch, and sat in the dark crying for hours. *You should have known better. What did you expect?*

Eventually, after many heart-to-heart talks, I forgave him. He tried to explain why he'd cheated. I listened.

"This shit ain't easy, Eb. Ever since I came home, I've been trying to make some shit happen and I keep getting doors slammed in my face. Shit with me and you wasn't working out, and then there's my family drama. I was depressed. The women were just an escape."

I don't know what it is, this place inside me that makes me

hold on, but it was all I knew to do. I wasn't sure anymore if I was staying because I was committed or, like my mama, I was too tired to do anything different, but I knew I loved him. Life together wasn't as easy as we'd hoped but I didn't want to lose him. I'd waited four long, hard years for him. *Four.* I'd invested too much.

I knew the pressure to succeed was consuming Shaka. He didn't have a job or a degree, the book business was still slow, and he had been piecing together work from consulting and speaking gigs. Then there was the guilt he carried because he hadn't been there to raise his son Jay, who was now struggling his way into manhood. Jay was bouncing from couch to couch with no real job or plan for his life. Shaka felt helpless. He had kicked it with him countless times about his life in the streets and the lessons he'd learned, but Jay was determined to do things his way. The sad irony—Shaka had poured himself into the young guys he'd mentored in prison, serving as a father figure to many of them, but couldn't seem to save the one person that mattered most, his own son.

When everything in his life seemed to be falling apart, I was Shaka's refuge. I had always been his refuge. I was heartbroken, but I knew the man I'd grown in love with was still there, buried beneath the pain.

Prison is a traumatic experience and it leaves innumerable scars. Shaka had always prided himself on the fact that prison didn't break him, that he was different. He thought once he came home all he needed was money and opportunity, but he needed more. So much more. He came home with scars he'd tried to mend, scars he didn't feel through all the toughness and the optimism, and I supported him the only way I knew how. But love wasn't enough.

With each secret I kept and stored away, I became invested in my silence. I thought that this is what *wise* couples do. They keep their business to themselves. And so I did.

I'd shared the news of Shaka's homecoming on social media when he first came home and my Facebook friends grew in love with our story. They rooted for us. When Shaka won the Black Male Engagement Leadership Award from the Knight Foundation, I shared the good news. When he got a fellowship at the MIT Media Lab, and then started teaching at the University of Michigan, I shared that news, too. But I couldn't share the not-so-pretty side of freedom. We were supposed to be the couple to prove prison relationships *can* work. Our success, proof that I wasn't crazy. If we didn't work out, that would mean I'd waited in vain; I'd been the fool my mama said I was. It would mean *I was wrong about him.*

And I couldn't be wrong. It was as if Shaka had been hand-picked just for me.

I tried to remember why I had fallen in love, heartbreak after heartbreak, year after year. I tried to convince myself that *this* is love.

62

'm ready to come home," Shaka announced one day out of the blue. "This dating shit ain't for me. Don't get me wrong, it's fun but it's not fulfilling."

"Are you sure?" I didn't want to get my hopes up.

"Yeah, these women can't touch you, Eb."

We immediately started making plans for Shaka to move back home. We had been inseparable the entire separation anyway. And we had Sekou. Reuniting our family just made sense.

Weeks before Shaka was set to move back in, I knew we had made a mistake—we weren't ready. The arguing never stopped. Even though we were apart, we hadn't given each other the space needed to process what had gone wrong in our relationship or do the work needed to heal old wounds. But the wheels were already in motion—Shaka had gotten out of his apartment lease three months early. *There's no turning back now.*

Things were rocky those first few weeks, then Shaka surprised me with a hot air balloon ride for my thirty-ninth birthday.

"Just pack an overnight bag. Bring something casual and something dressy."

"What you got up your sleeve?" I asked, blushing.

"All I can tell you is this is about to be the best birthday ever."

Shaka drove far outside the city and wouldn't give me any details no matter how many times I asked or tried to guess. When we pulled into the parking lot, I still didn't know where we were. And then I saw the big rainbow-checkered balloon sitting in the middle of a wide grassy field.

"Baby!" I screamed. I'd just written a bucket list, things I wanted to do before I turned forty, and riding in a hot air balloon was on it.

I am nervous and excited when we climb into the balloon's small basket, just big enough for six people and the pilot. The crew gives the pilot a thumbs-up and he turns on a propane burner. The balloon starts to fill up, and before I know it, the basket is lifted off the ground. We go up, up, up until we are nearly 5,000 feet in the air. The wind pushes us over lakes and trees and we see wildlife darting across the open woodlands below. Halfway into the hour-long flight, the pilot asks if anyone in our group of six wants to touch the treetops. "I do," I say, giddy. When he gives me the signal, I reach over the side of the basket.

"Aaahhhh!" I screamed as I grabbed a handful of leaves. "I got some!"

"Ayyeee," Shaka said, proud of me.

When we landed, I thanked Shaka repeatedly, still high off adrenaline. Afterward, we checked into an exclusive hotel in Birmingham for the night. When Shaka opened the door to our room, there were flower petals on the floor in a trail leading to the bed, and then more petals sprinkled on the sheets. There was champagne and chocolate-covered strawberries and cupcakes. I couldn't stop smiling.

Shaka was beaming the entire night. He'd talked so much about how he was going to show me how much he loved and appreciated me once he came home, and that night he delivered on his promise. I had never felt more special.

Weeks later we were back at it again.

"Did you send that email?"

"No, not yet. I'll do it today," I responded.

"You said that yesterday. Why don't you do it now?"

"I *said* I'll do it today," I snapped.

When we argued, I tried to remember those days in the visiting room leaning into each other, waiting on each other's words, hungry for each other's touch. Remember these moments, we said. Storms will come, we said. We are stronger than anything life throws at us.

I suggested we go to couples' counseling. Shaka hesitated but agreed. I did the research and returned with the names of some therapists I'd found online. "I'll think about it," he told me. Months later, still no therapist, I suggested we do some couples' exercises I'd discovered. "I'm just not in that space," he finally admitted. "I'm focused on building my dreams right now."

We had dug such a deep hole that climbing out seemed like a Herculean feat and his relationship muscles were tired. I hoped once Shaka got his first big win, he'd be able to give our relationship the time and attention it needed.

63

The proverbial straw that broke the camel's back started with an argument about the laundry—the bane of my existence. It may seem easy enough—sort the clothes, put them in the washing machine, then the dryer—but I hate doing laundry. I'm usually on my last pair of underwear before it dawns on me that it's time to wash. In college, I bought extra underwear and towels so I would have a longer runway when it came to washing clothes. Anything to get out of washing every week. Sometimes Shaka washed his own clothes when the pile in the corner of our bedroom became too much. That day he was frustrated. He was about to pack for a trip and didn't have any underwear.

The argument went south quick, and by the end of it we'd both shut down. He left the house without saying a word.

Once I put Sekou to bed, I cried out to God, *Is it finally time to let go?* I asked for a sign.

Later that night Shaka came home drunk and was out like

a light as soon as his head hit the pillow. I had spent the night tossing and turning, my heart heavy. I didn't know where he'd been, but a little voice said to check his phone.

I grabbed his phone even though I'd promised him I wouldn't look through it again. I went into the bathroom, closed the door, and sat on the toilet thumbing through his text messages. I was prepared for the worst but hoping to find nothing. My hands started trembling as I scrolled through text after text—he'd been cheating for months.

The screams stayed stuck in my throat. I thought about whether to wake Shaka up right then to confront him or go back to sleep. It would be a few hours before he roused from his drunken slumber. I lay in the bed beside him and wept, the queen-sized mattress suddenly feeling small.

What now? I thought to myself.

In that moment, God whispered to me, "Let go. I got you."

"But I can't. What about . . . ," I started, unsure of God's words.

"Trust me. This is just the beginning."

"But I thought you said . . . ," I continued, ready to list all the reasons why I couldn't let go.

"I did," God replied. "And now it's time to let go. I have more for you."

"But I don't know how to fly," I said, still unsure.

"You do, but you gotta let go first. I promise you won't fall. Trust me."

By morning, I had made up my mind. *I am moving.* I had no money saved, but I couldn't stay there, I kept telling myself. There were too many memories.

I confronted Shaka when he woke up and told him I was done.

"I looked through your phone," I started. I told him about the text messages I had read.

"Why you looking through my phone?" he replied, still rousing from his sleep. I looked into his eyes, searching for traces of the man I'd grown in love with.

This time I did not ask questions. The answers didn't matter, his words would feel empty, so I said nothing.

After I made Sekou breakfast, after I cleaned up the kitchen trying to busy myself, I started searching for an apartment. I browsed through a few rental sites, looking first for something nearby to make coparenting easier on us both. Then I remembered an apartment building in downtown Detroit that had been recently renovated. I'd always wanted to live downtown, so I called to schedule a tour.

I fell in love as soon as I walked into the apartment. It was beautiful. There was a band of windows all the way around the apartment with a spectacular view of the Detroit River and the Renaissance Center. But the rent was expensive, and with parking and utilities, it would stretch my budget further than I was comfortable. I weighed the pros and cons, and after talking to my brother who agreed to help me with the security deposit, I decided to go for it. I deserve this, I thought to myself.

I had always taken the safe route, calculating all the risks before making major life decisions. But this time I quieted that little voice in my head, the one that had a list of all the reasons why I shouldn't move into the apartment, and stepped out on faith.

That night, I cried again, freeing the tears I'd held all day. I didn't want to cry in front of Sekou. I knew he would ask, "Mommy, why are you crying?" and I didn't have an answer that would satisfy us both.

In the weeks that followed, I read the books of some of my favorite spiritual thinkers, I watched fifty-eleven inspirational talks and I lost myself in Sekou every chance I got.

The hopeless romantic in me had a million what-if scenarios on repeat in my mind. What if we'd gone to therapy? What if we'd stayed separated a little longer? What if we'd separated sooner? What if we'd tried harder? Eventually I came to understand that Shaka was being who he needed to be for me to grow.

In *The Power of Now*, Eckhart Tolle says that "whenever your relationship is not working, whenever it brings out the 'madness' in you and in your partner, be glad. What was unconscious is being brought up to the light," and it is in the light that I saw my childhood wounds.

The suffering was my own doing, resisting the natural flow of my life. The anxiety was the result of me trying to control what could not be controlled. Rather than let our relationship manifest the way it was meant, like water finding its way, I tried to force it.

Admitting the truth—that we were naïve, that love wasn't enough, that the system had won—was incredibly hard. I kept asking, "God, am I supposed to let it *all* go?" And I heard the answer, after much prayer and meditation. *Yes.* That meant releasing my attachment to the fairy tale. It meant releasing

Shaka from the promises he'd made, promises no man coming home from prison should make.

Two weeks later, I moved out of our Westland home and into what I hoped would be my sanctuary—a sacred space for me to heal, grow, and rebuild. It was a bittersweet moment. I was excited about beginning a new chapter, but all of this meant the end of a fairy tale. My whole life, my happily-ever-after, had been wrapped up in that fairy tale and now it was over.